THE
influencing
OPTION

THE
influencing
OPTION

The Art of Building

A Profit Culture

in Business

LIBBY WAGNER

GLOBAL
professional
publishing

Global Professional Publishing Ltd
Random Acres
Slip Mill Lane
Hawkhurst
Cranbrook
Kent TN18 5AD
Email: publishing@gppbooks.com

Global Professional Publishing Ltd believes that the sources of information upon which the book is based are reliable, and has made every effort to ensure the complete accuracy of the text. However, neither Global Professional Publishing Ltd, the authors nor any contributors can accept any legal responsibility whatsoever for consequences that may arise from errors or omissions or any opinion or advice given.

ISBN 978-1-906403-60-7

Contents

Dedication

To my parents, Jim and Virginia Wagner, who always encouraged my creative notions and insisted I have never been ordinary.

Introduction

A Poet Defines
a Profit Culture

I'm a poet and I've written this book for business leaders. There aren't that many of us, mostly because traditionally, poets don't know what to say to you and can't imagine how they might get through a cocktail party making small talk, much less be willing to enter into a boardroom to discuss your business strategy. And, frankly, many of you think poets are a little weird, sequestered in the dusty corners of a university campus, far from the technology building, talking about esoteric, metaphoric imagery. Or, we are wearing berets and hanging out in dark dive bars and coffee shops pontificating on the demise of humankind and reading weepy poems. We did not go to the same parties.

Besides, poets, in most western cultures, have taken some sort of martyrish approach to standing righteously outside the business arena, acting like we don't care and refusing to see the connections between you and us. In truth, we need each other[1]. In his oft quoted lines, William Carlos Williams, a physician and poet, said, "It is difficult/to get the news from poems/ yet men die miserably every day/for lack/ of what is found there," and though poets better than I have gone before (namely David Whyte)[2] to illuminate this dark space where we don't have the conversation about how we—the artists and the leaders of commerce—should cultivate our interdependence, I'll take the next step here.

Many times a year, now that I've left academia for good, I enter the metaphorical, literal boardroom. I go in from whence I came: as an advisor, teacher, and a student. I consult and advise and coach, primarily in the realm of organizational development, leadership, strategy, performance, and communication. I help my clients create *Profit Cultures*. Every good leader is the teacher and the student, always—the most maverick, the most innovative, the charismatic or the dull. In our quests as advisors and business leaders, we should, at the very core, be committed to growth—growth of the dendrites, the mind, knowledge, and society as a whole. The only other

---

1   See Dana Goia's article, "Can Poetry Matter?" in *The Atlantic*, May 1991.
2   Poet, author and advisor to organizational leadership. His book, *The Heart Aroused: Poetry and the Preservation of the Soul in Corporate America*, 1994, is a must-read.

choice is decay and decline. The business is just a microcosm of this—we grow, thrive, flourish and prosper, in small and large ways, or we diminish and die. There is no judgment here; there is a lifecycle of business and organizations just as any other life form, and if we choose to use our leadership power for good—for growth and profit—we can also create an organizational culture that supports it.

I was too loud for academia—my personality and my spirit. Spending almost 18 years there, believing in education utterly, loving the great gift of the synthesis of student learning, discourse and debate, my entrepreneurial spirit was only sated via permissive mentors and tolerant administrators. I created, I innovated; I did crazy things like teaching people to write and rock climb at the same time, taught poetry workshops in prison, directed *The Vagina Monologues*, ran committees and groups. I hated the meetings, the glacially-paced bureaucracies, the endless processing and repetitive discussion. Although several thought I might make a good college president, and I took advantage of the leadership development and internship positions, there was something deep inside that moved my own inner compass away from campus. Just because I *could* do something, didn't mean I *should*. I share this not because it's particularly significant except that the path I started out on isn't the path I finally ended up on, which for me is absolutely exactly as it should be. It's often not a straight route for any of us, regardless of vocation. This allows us to see many worlds. And, I'm here to share a secret: the inner world of the poet is not so different from the inner world of the leader because above all else, each has a human journey where in exchange for our ideas, observations and the work of a life, we simply want to make a difference for our having been here.

What, then, can a poet tell you about impacting your bottom line, your profits, however you may define that? First, it's important to define *Profit Culture* as we will examine it throughout the book. *A Profit Culture is an environment in which people work together to create positive outcomes for their organization or groups:*

- In corporations or for-profit businesses, their revenues are such that the bottom line is abundant: the money in exceeds the money out.
- In a non-profit or charitable organization, they utilize funding sources, grants and volunteerism, as well as other means, to successfully fulfill the mission.
- In government or civic groups, they utilize public monies to uphold their particular responsibilities, being good stewards of the public faith.
- In family or small businesses, professional and personal needs are met with excess left over to contribute to the consumer base, i.e. support other businesses via purchase of goods and services.

In other words, a Profit Culture is any organizational culture of abundance where people are engaged in growth-related activities to support the economic interchange. They create, they innovate, they shift and change, they might even scale back—but all activities and decisions ideally support some sort of contribution to the common good, including the good of the organization, its employees, customers and suppliers. A Profit Culture is also sustainable because it is ethical, high integrity, and strives to operate on high principles. A *profitable business* is not necessarily a sustainable Profit Culture, and we have many examples of boom and bust businesses, breaches of ethics and shady dealings—none of these will last because they do not have the human culture to support them.

How would you know if you encountered a Profit Culture? First, depending upon the kind of organization, a Profit Culture would fit the definition of those listed in the bulleted list, above. You do not have to be a for-profit business or a corporation. Profit, defined, includes not only the excess of income over expenditure, but also that some benefit or advantage has been gained via the interaction or exchange. Any organization can be a Profit Culture because it's really about having more than enough—to have abundance enough to create some good in some way. Other common characteristics of a Profit Culture include:

- Sense of hope, excitement or passion about organization's purpose
- Positivity
- Creativity
- Innovation
- Resilience
- Loyalty and faith
- Sense of helpfulness and generosity

Many leaders, past and present, focus on things in their organization that will not positively impact their revenues and growth, or their profitability. They're not stupid; they are acting out of the best intentions and the knowledge they have available. However, obsessive focus on the "bottom line" won't give you what you want because although the "bottom line" has been seen as synonymous with profits and profitability, the bottom line is at the bottom . . . it is the outcome of everything else that came before it. A Profit Culture starts way before your CFO or accountant can calculate your balance sheet. The "bottom line" is only one data point that reflects your leadership and one measurement of who you are, what you do, and the kind of influence you have exerted far upstream.

How can you lead and *influence* a Profit Culture? How can you build or create an organizational environment where the people who work there are highly engaged, innovative, creative and loyal? How can you attract the best customers, business partners and new employees to join your team? How can you differentiate yourself in the market, actually execute a brilliant strategy, *and* be happy in your work?

Let's begin with *you*.

Chapter 1

Leading in a Profit Culture: Creating a Success Mindset First

Want to or have to?

I was married once, for a short time, to a man who had five children. It seemed like a good idea at the time. As one might suspect, becoming insta-mom had its challenges. I, as a perfectly smart thirty-something woman, took on a persona I'd never seen before. I became hyper-vigilant, super-organized and paranoid about pattering feet in the night. I was overwhelmed by my new role and unaccustomed to its responsibilities and implications. I began to say all the things we remember as children our parents saying that we swear we won't. Instead of feeling some strange bliss of motherhood—after all, I had not given birth to any of *these people* ages seven to seventeen—I was overcome by my Position Power and protective of my turf where they would descend *en masse* every other week. My propensity for reasonableness diminished and I resorted to "because I said so!" to try to influence anything that might resemble order, a meal without disruption, or conflict over who got to ride shotgun on the way into town. I sought solace in the upstairs bathroom visualizing how I had managed to get myself into this minivan mania.

Although some may argue that leading an organization is not the same as leading a family, leading any group has commonalities because you are ultimately trying to get everyone going in the same direction with as little fuss, chaos and strewn body parts as possible. Whether you're heading a table, rallying the troops, or running the board meeting, there are some divine principles at work—you're trying to get them to come with you, and you're trying to do so to reach the goal or the vision of the group with as much effectiveness and perhaps efficiency as you can muster. No one sets out to be a controlling boss or parent; our intentions are good. However, we often become *exactly* the boss or parent we say we don't like and wonder how we got there.

Part of the trick is that people follow you for one of two reasons—they have to or they want to—and what you do largely determines which course they take and ultimately how challenging or easy it is to lead them. Your ability to create strong, powerful relationships will have a direct impact on your success and the success of your group or organization because when you have done your work up front—when you have rallied your troops and mounted your trusty steed—they will follow *you,* not the horse or the company or the minivan.

Why do we care why someone follows us just so long as they're back there? I don't know about you, but I'd like to know that we're not only moving in the same direction—toward the goal or vision—but also not be worried about people taking expensive, timely side trips. I'd like to know that even when I'm not physically there, people are still moving in the same direction and not wandering off on rabbit trails. The only way to ensure this is to create long-term commitment rather than simply settling for short-term compliance, and frankly, it takes less work from you in the long run. How much time, energy and resources have you spent chasing the minimally committed? How long does it take to negatively impact an organization or group when its members are not aligned and not following your vision of leadership? Official leadership comes with the authority and power of position—you're the boss or the manager or the supervisor and now you have the *right* to tell people what to do. You have control. You hold the destiny of the company and its workers in *your hands.* Some relish this—"Yeah!" one sergeant told me, "My stripes mean I can kick ass and take names!" Alternately, some may be ready to seek solace in the upstairs bathroom.

All of us have experienced leaders drunk with power. Tyrannical, dictatorial behavior is the stuff that makes history, changes cultures and civilizations, and has devastated thousands of lives—and I'm not just talking about world leaders making their mark for the books. This book isn't about the potential corruption of power—this book is about how you can ethically, respectfully lead from the front and influence others to follow you for the long haul. This is about how to develop your skills and make choices that will ultimately impact your success, your organization's success, and your followers' success. This is about how the intentions and behaviors you choose will ultimately determine whether or not you can build a Profit Culture to last. This is also, dare I say, about happiness—about relishing your role as a leader and minimizing your distress of herding all those cats, clouds, or whatever because you know that you can get people to follow you because they want to. You can create influencing power. You can do this without conflict or pain.

Following Someone You Want to Follow

What happens when people follow a leader they want to follow? Think about someone you followed or would follow because you wanted to—because you believed in the person, in the mission or goal. Why did you feel this way? What did the leader do to create a situation where you were willing to demonstrate commitment through your actions? Chances are high that if you've followed someone like this you did so because you believed that the person operated from a central point of integrity, or perhaps you believed that person had your best interests in mind, or maybe you had the common ground of both being committed to something greater than the two of you—a group's mission—and that increased your commitment to the leader you followed. We follow people we can believe in. We follow people who are willing to demonstrate courage and honor and who are willing to do the hard work of leading. If you are following someone you want to follow in an organization, how can that impact the bottom line? When good leaders align their people with their visions, all elements of an organization are impacted—profits, customer service, productivity, morale, repute, retention and innovation. In other words, the value is priceless.

Following Someone You Have to Follow

What happens when people follow leaders only because they have to? Not only do you get simple short-term compliance, which requires leaders to constantly revisit giving direction, constantly monitor performance and constantly manage interpersonal conflict and strife, but also you get anything from the walking retired to the maliciously compliant. People watch the clock, cordon themselves off, create silos and bureaucratic processes, tie themselves in knots, become distracted by any and everything not related to the goals and mission of the organization. They are reticent to take risks, be creative or innovative, save the company money or help their co-workers. At the best, they do just their jobs and they go home. There is no growth, no loyalty, no commitment. Sometimes, they leave, creating a loss of intellectual capital and organizational wisdom, disruption to the work flow and expense for rehiring. With all these potential costs, why then, do we continually resort to "because I said so!" and "kicking ass and taking names?"

Doing Better

Maya Angelou said, "When we know better, we do better," and we need to know better. And lest you think this book is about some sort of touchy-feely, leading-by-consensus, processing-to-death sort of model, let me assure you it's not. Good leadership is not for the faint at heart—it takes courage, chutzpa and fortitude. Good generals have sometimes suffered the ultimate price, and although that's an extreme example, they knew what their mission was and they got on the horse anyway. My father is a retired Air Force Lt. Colonel who served two times in the Vietnam conflict. Sometimes, I check with him about these leadership principles. "Dad," I'll say, "even when a great military leader has held all the cards for influencing, even when he can lead his troops to die and they *have to* follow him ..." "Yes," he's said, "they've built the loyalty of the troops. They follow the man."

What does it take to be the kind of leader that people *want* to follow? It's more powerful and simpler than you might imagine and it's not what they're teaching you in business school.

Developing a Success Mindset: Six Keys

Leading well involves leading yourself first. This seems an exercise in obviousness, though the simplest concepts can often be the most powerful. Leading yourself first means that you've got to start with you, on the inside, and that takes some courage and honesty. As I have worked one-on-one with many leaders in multiple industries, I have identified what I believe are Six Keys to developing a Success Mindset:

1. Self Confidence and Self Esteem
2. Getting over Yourself
3. Committing to Congruence
4. Removing Obstacles with Discipline and Perseverance
5. Balancing Accountability and Respect
6. The Differentiation Factor

Key 1: Self Confidence and Self Esteem

If you're a leader, don't you, by default already have healthy self confidence and self esteem? Not necessarily. And don't confuse ego or arrogance with confidence. Confidence suggests that you know what you know, and you also know you always have something to learn. Arrogance suggests you think you know it all and don't have anything much to learn. Self-esteem is related to your belief system, and especially your beliefs about yourself and how your own self-talk can help or hurt you. For our purposes, examine the following figure:

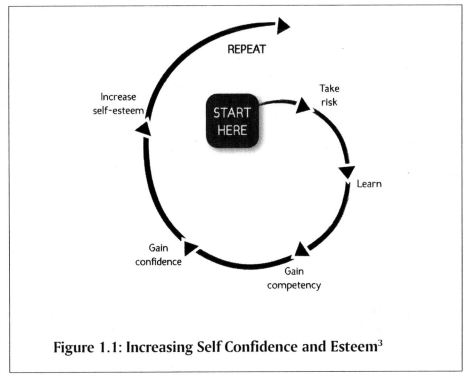

Figure 1.1: Increasing Self Confidence and Esteem[3]

As you can see, the critical piece here is to take a risk—a small risk, baby step, the one next thing that will lead you toward increased competence, which then positively impacts your confidence and thus your self-esteem. Wash. Rinse. Repeat.

The reason that self-confidence and self-esteem are so critical to your leadership success is that when you are self-confident, you can do three things much better than the average person: manage your time, say "yes" to the things you need to say "yes" to and say "no" to the things you need to say "no" to. This is a critical differentiation.

Key 2: Getting Over Yourself

I love to tell the story of my flippant answer to colleague and friend Wes Trochlil[4] when he called me to ask me what my goals were for attending my first Million Dollar Consulting College®. "I'm going to work really hard at getting over myself," I said, probably because I was tired, wasn't sure, and knew I was just going to spend

---

3   Adapted from an ALan Weiss model shared at workshop in Providence, Rhode Island, December 2008: *Self-Esteem Workshop: Do You Have Enough Self-Esteem to Attend?*

4   President, Effective Database Management, LLC. http://www.effectivedatabase.com/

a lot of money going to this workshop and I wasn't feeling very confident. The funny thing was, that was exactly what I needed to do to move to the next level of my success—and what many of the leaders I work with need to do: get over yourself.

On the one hand, getting over yourself is about having the self-confidence not to be so self-absorbed. It's knowing that the "80% and Go!" rule works, and that leading well, being successful is not about perfection. Getting over yourself is about eliminating self-sabotaging behaviors like procrastination, as well. On the other hand, getting over yourself is also about helping others, focusing on them—your subordinates, peers, colleagues, customers, suppliers, vendors, superiors—and how you can help them succeed, which can create the positive energy we need to lead. Getting over yourself is also, ultimately, about having a sense of humor about all this. It's just not that serious. You're going to make mistakes—learn from them and move on!

Key 3: Committing to Congruence: Take the Road Less Traveled—the High One

Elsewhere we are going to talk more about congruence, integrity and Presume Good Intent, so I won't spoil it here. However, right now you need to make your own commitment to epitomize integrity in all of your actions and interactions as a leader. You need to make a decision to take the high road, always. *Integrity* suggests the notion of integration and congruence. Who you are on the inside— your intentions—fully integrate with what happens on the outside—your actions. Recognize when discord might occur and make decisions about your personal deal-breakers in terms of ethics and honesty.

Recognize an important principle about influencing with integrity and leading a Profit Culture—

> *It is my behaviors that influence, not my intentions.*

That statement, simple as it is, is worth rereading—so many leaders begin with the greatest of intentions, they may even be able to tell you about their great intentions, but when their actions and behaviors don't match up, when they say they believe in teamwork and respect but they're yelling in sales meetings and threatening people in the hallways, it simply doesn't work. It's tough to regain credibility after it's lost. Behaving with integrity takes discipline and self-awareness. The models for communicating, leading and influencing presented in the following chapters simply won't work unless you can utilize the tools while operating from absolute integrity. Period.

Key 4: Removing Obstacles with Discipline and Perseverance

Sometimes, we can feel stuck, or as if there is simply something that we need to overcome in order to move more closely toward the goal or outcome we desire. "Clear the Swamp[5]" is a tool that we use with clients to help them identify the obstacles to motivation for teams and groups. You can also perform a mini "Clear the Swamp" on yourself by asking this question: "What are the current issues, obstacles or problems that are preventing me from _____?" You fill in the blank with where you want to go: the next level of success, the next goal on the list of goals, your next position, etc. Then the important thing to do is try to identify both real and imagined obstacles because sometimes we perceive that something is an obstacle, and we create a whole story about why we can't overcome it, when in reality, it's not as bad as we think it is. Sometimes, we need a coach, mentor, or advisor to help us work through obstacles, but not investigating them will keep us stuck. In addition, when we persevere, we are balancing both the determination to see something through to its finish and knowing when enough's enough. It is not a dogged pursuit of a losing battle, but rather the conviction to keep moving forward toward our goals, one step at a time.

Key 5: Balancing Accountability and Respect: Are you Tipping the Scale in Your Favor?

Let's be honest about honesty right up front. When I'm working with leaders, we have to talk about honesty and candor. In Jack Welch's *Winning,* he notes candor as one of the most essential qualities of a leader and indeed one of the most rare. *Why?* Why are candor and honesty so difficult for leaders, for organizations and their people, especially when you can get everyone in the room to agree that honesty is in their top-five most favorite values—nobody says, "*nah*—honesty is overrated!"

This model for leadership and influencing, designed to help you build a Profit Culture, is based on honesty. This honesty is direct, specific, succinct and without fluff. This honesty is also ethical and aware. Frankly, if there were more honesty like this around, I would have much less work to do as a consultant. We spend so much time dancing around honesty, avoiding the evidence and truth, we cost our organizations millions of dollars and countless hours of stress and loss of productivity.

---

5   See Chapter 5

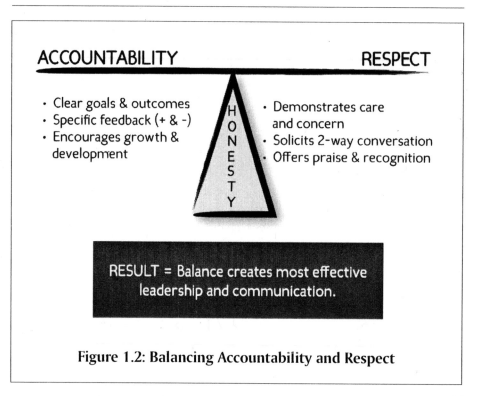

Figure 1.2: Balancing Accountability and Respect

Here's the trick, the most effective delivery of an honest message *balances both accountability and respect*, especially if the target of our honesty is someone whom we'd like to influence to change, to encourage followership, and especially if what we're trying to do is to create long-term commitment rather than short-term compliance. It *does* matter how the message is delivered. There is a difference between respectful honesty and disrespectful honesty.

Cost of Disrespectful Honesty: Being Brutally Honest

Let's examine the costs of disrespectful honesty. Some people like to take pride in the fact that they will tell you the truth. "I'll be brutally honest with you," is a common phrase we might hear. How about just being honest and leaving out the "brutal" part? This is really just a preview to tell you that they are going to tell you the truth, but they don't care if it hurts your feelings, devalues you, or damages the relationship. But, since they told you up front they were going to be brutal, it's okay? *Rubbish*, as my friends in the U.K. say!

For example, you have someone on your team who is simply not performing. This lack of performance, lack of sharing the work of projects is beginning to impact all the things important to your team—deadlines, success, customer service, team cohesiveness. You need to influence her to change—now! You need to be candid, and the language you choose will impact not only the short-term result but also even more importantly, the long-term outcome of your team. Do you tell her she's lazy, ineffective and selfish to expect her team members to carry her load while she's taking extended lunches with her girlfriend in the next office? Do you shame her into feeling guilty that you've been working such long hours to pick up the slack for her lack of action? *You can*—and all of those things might feel true to you about the situation, but chances are you'll get a defensive person whose trust in you is diminished and who now moves into the likelihood of short-term compliance, if she moves at all. This is an imbalance of accountability and respect.

Too Heavy: Accountability

Consider this imbalance—when someone is really *heavy* on the demonstration of accountability—they hold you to deadlines and specific details, direct and follow-up

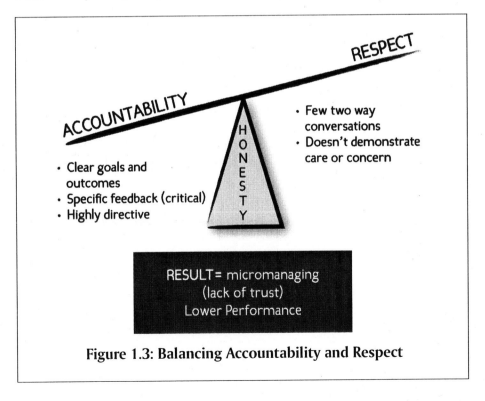

Figure 1.3: Balancing Accountability and Respect

on your work, monitor your progress—but *light* on demonstrating respect to you—they don't answer questions, listen to concerns, value your ideas or input, speak to you with courtesy—what's the result? You feel micromanaged, undervalued and perhaps even abused. You are more likely just to do the minimum and feel resentful about it because your leader is not showing any respect to you.

Can You Have Too Much Respect?

On the other hand, what if the opposite occurs? A leader whose behaviors consistently demonstrate respect—listening to concerns, answering questions, offering explanations, caring about you as a person, asking for your input or feedback—but who doesn't hold you accountable, creates an equally undesirable result—nothing gets done! Eventually, you lose respect for this person because there is this imbalance between accountability and respect. It's not that complicated—most people just want to do a good job and feel like their work means something. They want to be both respected and held accountable.

If you are willing to be honest and specific about your expectations, yet firm

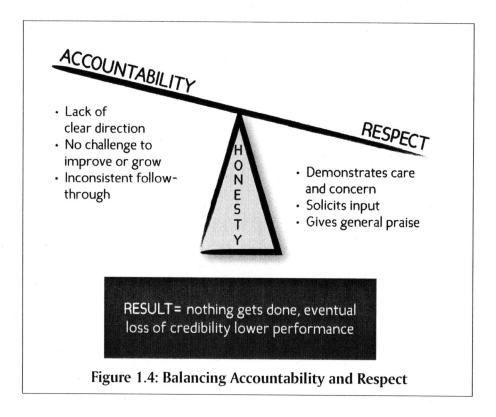

Figure 1.4: Balancing Accountability and Respect

and respectful in your delivery, your chances of increasing trust and increasing commitment are greater. If you are able to address your team member, one-on-one, with respect, and ask for exactly what you want—her demonstrated commitment to the team by meeting deadlines, finishing projects and helping co-workers—you are being respectfully honest. And, importantly, you both have a chance of winning—it's not a zero sum game. The bonus is that when we are willing to develop our balance of accountability and respect, we earn the trust and respect of those who follow us. They know you will hold them accountable; they know you will do so respectfully. Hard to argue with that. Portions of this book will guide you through how to have such a conversation—or confrontation—balancing accountability and respect on the fulcrum of honesty. The leader who knows how to do this effectively is a rare leader indeed and one whose effectiveness to influence followers is greatly increased.

Key 6: The Differentiation Factor[6]

In my work with hundreds of leaders—big companies, small companies, organizations, agencies and teams—two particular elements differentiate the effective, successful leaders from those who struggle and strain in their ability to influence their followers. You may be surprised at their simplicity. Or maybe not. You may think, "well, everyone knows that!" but *knowing* and *doing* are different and I'm going to tell you that much more doing should be happening out there. Here they are:

> **Differentiator 1**: Clearly articulate your vision and get others to follow.
> **Differentiator 2**: Confront issues quickly, directly and respectfully.

Recognizing the simplicity of these differentiators, I wish I could tell you that leaders' ability to successfully implement them was high—that the Differentiation Factor was a rarity. I wish I could tell you that leaders have got this down pat and have time to dream big dreams and deal with global implications. Instead, I find over and over that the negative impacts of not implementing the Differentiation Factor leads to problems in productivity, trust, morale, retention, profits, customer service—all the things that keep leaders up at night, searching the shelves at Barnes & Noble, and hiring expensive consulting firms.

---

6   See "Two Strategies for Succes" by Libby Wagner which appeared in American Management Association's *MWorld*, September 2007.

Differentiator 1: Clearly articulate your vision[7] and get others to follow you.

No matter the industry, I find two main errors in thinking when it comes to the vision/mission/values issue: either there is none articulated at all, or it's so vague no one believes it's important enough to impact the actual work of the business. Companies take their executive team out to the woods to hash out lengthy, unwieldy descriptions of what their companies are trying to do. Often, they are exhausted by the effort and less than happy with the results.

Sometimes, they roll out their work to lukewarm reception only to have their own enthusiasm fizzle as the day-to-day operations and firefighting take precedent over fulfilling any plaque on the wall or inscripted post-its. Or, executives make the mistake of thinking, "Hey, we hire professionals—they're grown-ups. They know what to do and how to behave," which leads to all sorts of potential problems.

Here's the thing: your employees believe that you have the vision in mind and they think it's your job to tell them about it. It is! It is of the utmost importance. Remember that the degree to which you are not specific, someone has to guess or to try to read your mind. You won't be happy with the results and neither will your team or organization.

If you have a clearly articulated vision, and you've demonstrated high levels of specificity by giving enough information for people to be successful, then you must influence[88] others to follow. The key here is in identifying alignment—how can you create a clear line between the organization's vision, the team's mission, and the individual's goals? Influencing others involves creating buy-in and commitment, increasing trust in an organization, and illustrating what's in it for them. Answering the WIIFM (What's in it for me?) question is essential—don't leave it up to chance, and don't assume the WIIFM answer is that the person gets to keep his job! That's not enough to create loyalty and long-term commitment and it's not enough to engender effective influencing.

Differentiator 2: Confronting[9] issues quickly, directly and respectfully.

I would venture to say that ineffective confrontation skills are one of the top causes of pain, dissent, and distraction in organizations. Leaders need to respond thoughtfully and immediately to issues that arise that may impact business results—

---

7   Check out Chapter 4, a whole chapter devoted to articulating your vision!

8   Chapters 6 and 8 have specific tools for influencing.

9   Chapter 9 will help you confront effectively.

interpersonal conflict, performance issues, stalled team processes, poor ethics, breaches in customer service. Candor and honesty are the important currency of good leadership—the art is in the delivery.

Ineffective confrontation is often volatile, blaming. It is not future-focused and, instead, often damages the relationship between the leader and the other person. It creates *wreckage*. It is helpful if you are willing to redefine *confrontation* as someone's ability to respectfully resolve an issue—it does not have to be *confrontational*. Effective confrontation is direct, specific, and respectful. It is the perfect execution of the balancing act mentioned before—holding people accountable while demonstrating respect. Effective confrontation can actually increase trust in a relationship and decrease defensiveness—it goes hand-in-hand with effective influencing skills and helps to create an atmosphere of commitment, accountability, and teamwork.

Where Do We Go From Here?

If the goal, as demonstrated in figure 1.4, is to build and lead a Profit Culture, as you become a more effective leader, you can see how these elements build upon each other.

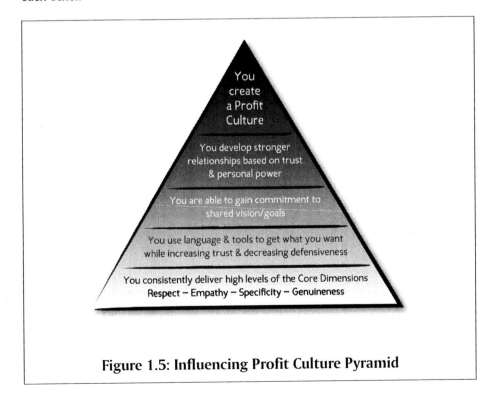

Figure 1.5: Influencing Profit Culture Pyramid

Level 1: You are consistently delivering high levels of the Core Dimensions to create a strong foundation for trust. (See Chapter 3)

Level 2: You are using language and tools to influence and actually increasing trust in the process while decreasing obstacles, such as defensiveness. (See Chapters 6, 7 and 8)

Level 3: You are able to gain commitment to shared vision and/or goals to increase the foundation for influencing. (See Chapters 4 and 5)

Level 4: You have developed strong relationships based on trust and personal power. (See Chapters 3, 5 and 8)

Level 5: You are continuing to become a more effective influencer cultivating the environment for your profit culture. (See Chapter 10)

How can Chapter 1 help you build and influence a Profit Culture?

Becoming a leader others want to follow involves leading yourself first by embracing the Six Keys to a Success Mindset These principles and practices begin to set the foundation for the coming tools and techniques. Start with you.

Chapter 2

Giving Yourself Permission and Holding Yourself Accountable

Defining Your Leadership Voice

Bessie Stanley, *on success:*

> *"To laugh much; to win the respect of intelligent persons and the*
> *affections of children; to earn the approbation of honest critics*
> *and endure the betrayal of false friends; to appreciate beauty;*
> *to find the best in others; to give one's self; to leave the world*
> *a little better, whether by a healthy child, a garden patch, or*
> *a redeemed social condition; to have played and laughed with*
> *enthusiasm, and sung with exultation; to know even one life*
> *has breathed easier because you have lived—this is to have*
> *succeeded."*

Leadership: An Inside Job First

First, and truly most importantly, if you want to create a Profit Culture, you must know who you are as a leader, what is important to you, what your ideals are, your boundaries, your inner rules for operating. You can't do this work on the surface of yourself because everything you are—your hopes, dreams, experiences, beliefs, paradigms—will all determine how you show up.

Over and over again people want to know whether leaders are born or made. It's not a silly question, though examining your purpose or mission as a leader will tell you a little about whether you've got some natural talents or abilities, and whether you want to develop yourself as a leader. My belief is that people are somehow called to be leaders, they emerge as leaders, and then they are cultivated, developed, and grown. If we're lucky (or purposeful in finding one), we have a mentor who takes an interest in us, and they help us. If not, we can get started on our own with a sincere desire to help. Much has been examined about servant leadership, service-oriented leadership, and lately Margaret Wheatley, author of *Leadership and the New Science*, has spoken about a shift from hero-based leadership to host-based leadership. There are many paradigms, and the one I am going to share throughout this book is the one that I see that works most often, for the long-term.

I don't think a leader can lead without knowing him- or herself first. Sometimes, as a young leader, we are excited about making a difference, or we believe strongly in something, or we are enamored by the idea of authority and power—we want to make the decisions and steer the direction. Many leaders actually mature into their roles, and this has nothing to do with age. Parents can probably understand best, how, in the taking on of raising children, each day you grow into a different version of yourself that you would've never known had you not been present for all of the learning that parenting brings. Leadership is like that, too.

Who Are You?

So, who are you? Why do you want to lead? What calls you to step forward, or say "yes!" or move into the light? Here are some of the most common reasons I see:

- A sincere desire to help an organization, cause, or group
- A sense of duty or devotion
- A drive to make a difference in the world
- A motivation to have a particular lifestyle for self, family and loved ones
- An attraction to challenging oneself or an ambition toward self-improvement

Most likely, at least one of the above rings true with you.

Voice and Style

At the risk of sounding clichéd, leaders come in all shapes, sizes and colors. They have varying styles, personalities and results. And honestly, this really cannot be encapsulated into some sort of categorization or profile: your Myers-Briggs® or DiSC® or "colors" assessments might offer an intriguing horoscope-like, lively discussion, but it's not truly *you*. Frankly, I've met some leaders whose colors are more akin to a Jackson Pollack painting. Leaders are complex and multi-layered.

What I believe differentiates you as a leader is your *voice*.

Your voice is the articulation and manifestation of who you are as a person and a manifestation of your character. I realized, after my consulting business had become successful, that I really was doing what I'd always done—helping people find their voices. As a teacher, I helped students find their voices in writing and speaking. Now, I work with leaders to help them get really clear about what they want, what they envision for their teams and organizations, and then we figure out how to "say" it out loud—in person, in text, in actions. Their leadership voices become stronger and more confident, as they become better influencers.

When I went to writing school, we learned about voice. What does this mean? You have something to say that's important. How or why people may believe you, be moved by you, and *especially moved to act*, is important. What does your voice sound like? Not necessarily its auditory characteristics, but the way people perceive what you are saying with language and without. How do you know if you've found your authentic voice and whether it will influence anyone or impact business results?

Voice is how you sound in your speech, your writing, your messaging and framing. Voice—in Core Dimensions[10] terms (see Chapter 3)—is the manifestation of Genuineness. Those behaviors and actions and idiosyncrasies that make you *you* and allow you to lead from a place of confidence, assurance and passion. Voice is weaving your stories and experience and view of the world into how you lead and how others perceive you. Your voice is uniquely, absolutely yours.

Most business writing I read is awful—boring, verbose and absolutely ignores the audience in any way other than to demonstrate how smart the author thinks he is. Many business leaders are using their leadership voices in the same way—without authenticity, stilted, dull. There are exceptions, of course, and these are those whose voice, personality and humanity jump out at you when you read. You feel like you know the person, have a sense of their style, personality and principles. They feel authentic and genuine to you. If what they say resonates with you, you might even imagine yourself aligning or following, adapting or adopting ideas, methodologies or traits. I think this is one reason why new web marketing technologists encourage people to utilize videos to market themselves—at least we can hear people, see them and what they might be like because often their voices "on the page" are difficult to discern.

---

10   The Core Dimensions—Respect, Empathy, Specificity and Genuineness—are the foundational behaviors for the Influencing Options model for communication and leading. Genuineness, or authenticity, is a key element in building trust.

I still help people find their voices: I help my clients identify what they want, why they want it, how to say it or ask for it, how to clearly articulate, how to listen and respond, how to make their own decisions—all of these things help someone stand firmly, decidedly, in their own important places, speaking with confidence. Where do you want to take your company or team? What does success look like for you? What do you want them to do, or stop doing? Your ability to articulate, to use language that rings true to you and that influences others, is using your voice well.

Steps to Refining Your Voice

Step 1. Get a journal, thought book or someplace to write and record your thinking.

Yes, I realize that paper is so *old school* and we're on the verge of "kindleing" becoming a verb, but I think it makes a difference. I can type really fast and I can write on a computer, too, but I know I write differently long-hand. It's kinetic in a different way. Just do it.

Step 2. Use the following questions to prompt your writing and thinking. Best method is to just write, without stopping, editing or censoring. If you struggle with writing or this whole idea sounds torturous, make it as easy as you can on yourself. I use a digital kitchen timer sometimes to help me stay focused for a period of time. If you get stuck, just write "I can't think of anything . . . " or "blah blah blah" until you get unstuck.[11]

1. WHAT DO YOU WANT? How do you envision your best version of yourself as a leader? Where would you work? With whom? In what industry or circumstances? Or perhaps less general, what do you want in a particular situation or scenario? In your current role?

2. WHY DO YOU DO WHAT YOU DO? What is your personal mission or purpose? What gets you excited and completely enthusiastic? Where is your passion? Where do you feel "whole-hearted?"

3. WHAT EXPERIENCES OR INCIDENTS HAVE SHAPED YOU? What are some of the best lessons you've learned? How do you know? What would you do again, no matter what?

4. HOW DO YOU MAKE THINGS BETTER? I've included, at the beginning of the chapter, one of my favorite Emerson quotes about defining success. How about you? What is your ultimate value and contribution?

---

11   If you love this already, you need to check out Natalie Goldberg's *Writing Down the Bones* and other books.

5. WHAT NEXT? Where do you go from here? What's your next step,
   decisive action or grand adventure?

Set your timer (or watch the clock) and write for at least 10 minutes on each topic without stopping. Don't be surprised if you want to write more—indeed, these are things that are important to you and you may have a lot to say!

Step 3: Put your writing/thinking work away for at least a day. Give yourself some distance from the idea generating and brainstorming.

Step 4: Then, set aside an hour or 90 minutes to review and reflect on what you've written. Ask yourself the following:

1. What themes do I see that seem important?
2. What is surprising or intriguing about what I wrote? Was anything missing that I thought would show up, but didn't?

Step 5: Then, complete the following:

After my review, I have identified the following three intentions for my own development as a leader:

1.

2.

3.

This writing/thinking exercise helps you get clear about what's important to you and for you. Reflecting and reviewing allows you to identify the next, most pertinent intentions to have for yourself. This is the road to congruence.

Congruence

Congruence is a desirable destination—it means that your principles, beliefs and intentions are matched up, integrated, with what you are doing and who you are being. I believe this is a source of joy, happiness and fulfillment. We know when the opposite occurs: when we are not congruent. We find ourselves exhausted, burned-out and frustrated. Why does congruence matter as a leader? Because when you are congruent, you are at your best. When you are congruent, your behaviors match your intentions and you are more effective, efficient and confident. Eventually, lack of congruence in a leader creates an obstacle for success in organizations.

In Real Life

At one point in my career, I had a job I really enjoyed. I worked with a dynamic team; we got along well together and experienced great success in our work. I was daily excited about the challenges and projects we worked on and that were on the horizon. I felt like I, along with my team, was truly making a difference. Part of my job included traveling to different sites to collaborate with other teams and help them launch new programs and engage their creativity. It was a lot of fun!

After two years, we were on the verge of launching a new program, when my family suffered a terrible loss and I was gone from work for several weeks. Upon my return, my bosses notified me that my job had changed focus and purpose. I was now working mostly alone, at my desk, on large deadline-driven projects. Each day, I dragged myself to the office. Each day, I bartered with myself, creating made-up deadlines and milestones: "just three more months," I'd say as I walked back to my cubicle. I was not congruent. I felt like I was wasting my talents and abilities, and I found very little joy in my workday or relationships. This was a toxic place for me to be. I was gone from this job in less than three months.

Being, Thinking and Doing

Leadership is all of the above: being, thinking, and doing. If *being* is the first step in congruence (knowing who you are), then *thinking* and cognition grow out of our beliefs. We can change and shape our thinking to support who we want to be as leaders and how we want to lead. *Doing*, of course, involves the actions and processes we enlist to facilitate things happening around us. Creating alignment among *being, thinking* and *doing* will help us to cultivate that congruence, or inner Genuineness.

Following are three very practical tools, based on some abstract concepts and models that I use successfully with leaders, and they, in turn, report that utilizing these simple tools helps to transform their leadership capabilities and satisfaction.

Tool 1: Presume Good Intent

This particular *thinking* tool causes all the cynics in the room to rise up and take notice.

> *Presume good intent? Are you crazy? I've known this guy for years and he's always trying to manipulate the situation for his benefit! He's thrown me under the bus so many times I've got the scars to prove it. There's **no way** I can Presume Good Intent with this guy!*

Even if all of that is true, and your experience with someone demonstrates a relationship that has low trust or a less-than-desirable dynamic, I'm still going to tell you that presuming good intent can work. Why? Because presuming good intent is not about the other person, it's about *you*. It's about how you show up to a situation and the impact your thinking will have on the outcome. Presuming good intent is probably two steps above giving someone "the benefit of the doubt," which according to my OED (*Oxford English Dictionary*), originated sometime in the 1800s and had appeared with reference to a court case—the person had been given "the benefit of the doubt" because the evidence was inconclusive and conflicting. But here, in our leadership situation, we're not talking court cases, we're talking about how to show up and use our thinking to our benefit as a leader.

Presuming Good Intent means this:

- Most people want to do the best they can.
- This person in front of me (or this group) believes that they are doing the right thing or making the best decision they can at the moment
- This person/group is operating out of a desire to further an objective that they believe serves them (or the group or team or you)

Often, when I am coaching executives who are struggling with a particular person—employee, partner, board member—and I suggest that one place to begin is to Presume Good Intent, I get a lot of raised eyebrows. Consider this: if, for the moment, you set your thinking upon the premise that this person, no matter how off-base or wrong you think she is, is trying to do her best, is operating according to what she believes is the best course of action, how would you interact with her? If, on the other hand, you think that she's ignorant, stupid, idiotic, lazy, out to get you, then how then do you interact with her? In other words, whatever you presume has an impact on how *you're* going to behave, what you're going to get, and how the results will impact the overall outcome.

In figure 2.1, you'll notice that typically, we see people through a filter—we have created a story we tell ourselves about them which sometimes stands in the way of not only presuming good intent, but also fully listening to them and being open.

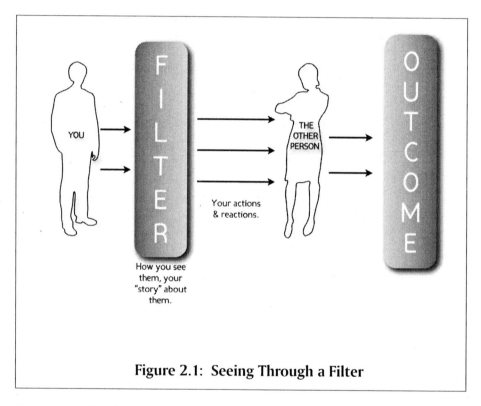

Figure 2.1: Seeing Through a Filter

Here's the basic rule:

1. Presume good intent
2. Listen openly
3. If you still get a negative feeling or intuition, check it out.
4. Investigate and re-frame, if necessary.

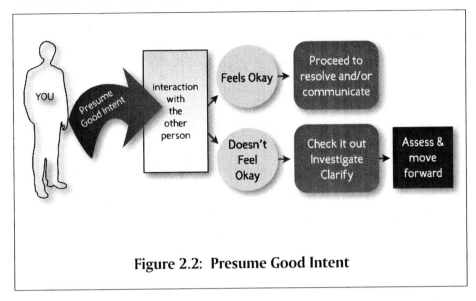

Figure 2.2: Presume Good Intent

In *Leadership and Self-Deception: Getting Out of the Box*, the authors from the Arbinger Institute use a parable to share some practical application of Presume Good Intent thinking, though they don't call it that. They use a model of "in the box" thinking and "out of the box" thinking and how this perception has a direct impact on not only your success but also the results you are trying to achieve. One of the most provocative concepts for me was that of "self-betrayal" and "collusion." You know the right thing to do, and when you deny this, you create a situation where you, perhaps unknowingly, enter into collusion with the other person to remain in self-deceptions. Most of the time "the right thing" is to stop focusing on yourself and be willing to be open to helping the other person.[12]

Einstein said, "the single most important decision a person will make is whether or not he believes the universe is friendly," and indeed this might be related to how you look at the world—positively or negatively, half-full glass or half-empty glass—and I've got a pretty strong conviction, based on extensive experience, about people who tout themselves as cynics or "realists." Cynicism is really a mask for fear of being disappointed, either for the first time, or again. Presuming Good Intent, being optimistic and hopeful, is, well, risky, isn't it? What if it doesn't work out? What if the person really isn't keeping your best interests, or the interests of the organization, in mind? What if . . . . ?

Presuming Good Intent takes courage, and that's why, in the end, it is about you and not about them.

---

12   I also like *Karmic Management: What Goes Around Comes Around in Your Business and Your Life*, by Roach, McNally and Gordon. 2009.

Tool 2: Frankl's Last Freedom

I'd like to mention Vicktor Frankl here for a few reasons. Anyone who has worked with me as a coach or consultant gets a book list of recommended resources, and on that list I always include Frankl's **Man's Search for Meaning**. Reported to be one of the ten most influential books of our time, Frankl's account of his experience in the concentration camps during World War II is legendary, and the examination of why people, when they experience a particular kind of stimuli, have such differing responses, led him to develop his distinct approach to psychotherapy, *logotherapy*.

Basically, Frankl suggested that there is a space between the stimulus of something that happens and our response to that stimulus.

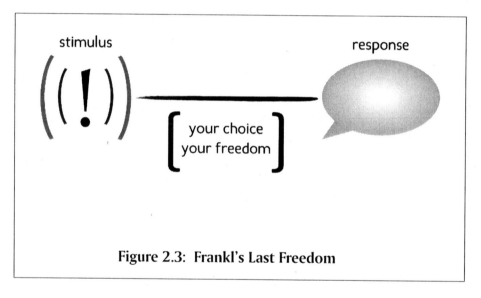

Figure 2.3: Frankl's Last Freedom

In that space in time, no matter how big or small, long or short, we get to choose how we will respond to what has happened to us and in this, as those who suffered the experience of the camps, we have the *freedom* (perhaps the last real freedom) *to choose* our response. It's easy to see how Frankl might deem this "the last human freedom," since his experiences before release from Auschwitz certainly afforded him the observation of many different people, in sometimes devastating circumstances, who were able to choose how they might interpret, respond and transcend those circumstances. Additionally, the ability to choose does not mean you negate the happening, but rather that you, in your free will, your own mind, get to select how you might move forward from that experience: devastation, depression, acknowledgement, hope, understanding—all are options available to you.

What does this have to do with leadership and defining your leadership voice? You, too, have the ability to choose your response in whatever happens. Your ability to deal with good news, bad news, conflicting information, change, disappointment, etc. sets that tone you are trying to achieve in your organization when all eyes are on you as the leader. Your ability to facilitate problem-solving, deal with a crisis, make tough decisions all stems from how you perceive what's happening and how you take advantage of the space between stimulus and response. Granted, and Frankl suggests this, that your past experiences, perhaps personality development and your environment have shaped the current patterns of belief and common responses you might have to something; however, and this is what is really important, you can choose, in that moment, to do something different from what you've done in the past, especially if you don't think it's working for you or hasn't been effective for you in the role of leader.

Tool 3: Three Effective Options, and One More

In the Influencing Options® model for communicating and influencing, we introduce the Three Options (or sometimes called the Three Choices) model. In actuality, there are four options, but only three of these are effective and will contribute to the congruence and effective leadership behaviors we've been examining.

Here's how the Three Choices work:

First, let's say you have something that has happened that is causing you distress of some kind. This can be mild: annoying, irritating, inconvenient—or it can be strong: really stressful, interrupting sleep or eating and causing great anxiety. Anywhere along that continuum we may experience something as distressful:

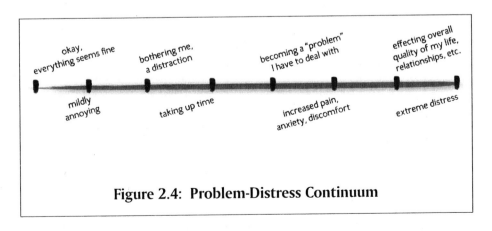

Figure 2.4: Problem-Distress Continuum

At the point we recognize that we've got this problem, or thing that's causing some degree of distress, we basically have three effective options:

1. **Influence**: choose to influence the situation by doing something to change the external circumstances.
2. **Acceptance**: choose to accept the situation by creating an internal change or shift—a letting go.
3. **Removal**: choose to remove ourselves either from the situation entirely, especially if it's a deal-breaker and goes against our values and principles, or choose to place specific boundaries around the situation or relationship so that it has minimal negative impact on us (sometimes called mini-removal).

Let's examine each in more detail, talk about the costs of each, and use some examples:

Choosing to Influence

Choosing to influence means that you decide it's worth it to you to try to change something about the situation. This situation is important enough that you are willing to risk the following (or pay the price) to try to create change. Some potential costs of influencing are:

- Your own courage and emotional fortitude
- You might make the situation worse; there's no guarantee
- The relationship might suffer or the person might say "no."

Choosing to influence is about taking action of some sort—having a conversation, writing a letter, doing something to try to bring about change.

Choosing to Accept

Sometimes people get confused about acceptance because they do two things: translate it into a loss of some sort (i.e. I wanted something and now I'm giving up, therefore I lose.) or they will say they accept something but still whine, moan, groan and complain about it. Acceptance means that, after purposeful examination, you decide it's simply not worth it to put forth the effort to influence, and you don't want removal. In other words, the internal shift you experience might sound something like this: *I have looked at my options and decided that I'm not going to let this issue take up any more negative space in my thoughts, feelings or time. I'm letting it go and moving on.*

And then you do—move on and let go. Acceptance can be a great relief and a very healthy response to the churning and worry we can sometimes get caught up in when something's bothering us. Knowing who you are, what's important to you and who you are as a leader helps you know when Acceptance is the right choice for you.

Choosing to Remove

Sometimes, Removal is seen as a non-option because it feels so radical. *I can't quit my job or leave this family . . . !* Well, you *can*, but the cost may be too high for you and therefore it's not the best option for you. What happens often, however, is that we forget we not only have this option, but also that we can choose varying degrees of it to get unstuck.

Have you ever left a job or a relationship because it just wasn't working for you? Looking back now, how do you feel about that choice? Most people can relate to this, and again, it's not about "losing" in the sense that you couldn't take it, or you were weak, so you decided to remove yourself. Choosing removal from an empowered, strong position is not only incredibly effective, it's one sign of a healthy psyche and effective person. Sometimes, it's time to go.

Sometimes, in the case of a job or important relationship, you may feel that the cost of removing yourself is too great and you choose to stay—you still have Acceptance or Influence as alternatives. On the other hand, you may decide that Removal *is* the best thing for you. Remember, the choice you make is yours and dependent upon many factors that are important to you. What often happens, when people feel trapped or stuck in a job that doesn't seem to fit or an unhappy relationship, is that they continue to feel worse and worse, increasing the movement to the right on the distress continuum. Know your "deal breakers" and this will help you identify whether or not Removal is a viable option for you. Generally, deal breakers are those issues related to your values and principles, such as:

- Ethics
- Honesty
- Integrity
- Respect for person or property
- Health and wellness

Knowing your boundaries is important because it empowers you to make the best choices for yourself. For example, if you were asked to engage in an unethical or dishonest practice in a company, you may choose to leave that job rather than stay and pay the cost of doing something that goes against your values and sense of integrity. OR, if you have a friendship with someone who is repeatedly dishonest with you, you may choose to end that friendship rather than suffer the cost of continued exposure to low levels of the Core Dimensions (Respect, Empathy, Specificity and Genuineness) with that person. *It's your choice.* Removal can be one of the most dramatic options, but it is always a choice you have.

You may also choose something a little less radical: a mini-removal, where you choose to limit your interactions or exposure to the person or situation that is causing the distress. We might ask for a transfer, or simply minimize the time we spend with that person or on that team or committee. If we think "radical" removal is too costly, we can choose this one instead.

The Other One

The only other choice, if we don't select to Influence, Accept or Remove, is to choose to remain distressed, unhappy or frustrated. Over time, this can lead to increased levels of stress, miserable-ness, depression, anxiety, negativity, pessimism, burnout, and we get sick. In Influencing Options® we call this The Toxic Zone.

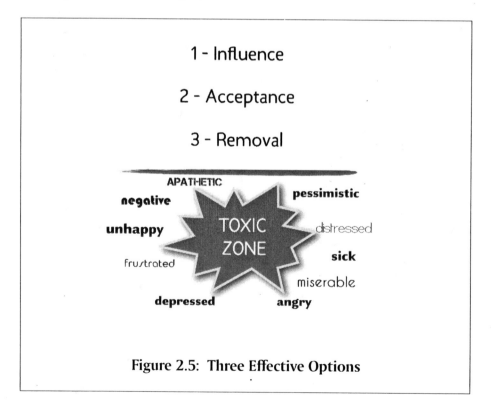

Figure 2.5: **Three Effective Options**

I always say we might visit the Toxic Zone on cranky days or distressful moments, but it's not okay to pitch a tent or build a condo. And, frankly, we all know people who do. What they take on, by selecting this choice (and it is important to remember that *it is a choice!*) is a victim mode or victim stance: *I am powerless to choose. I'm a victim to this person, organization, town, country . . .*

Sometimes, we do feel stuck, and the distress or change is causing high anxiety, but if we remember the following, we can not only increase our own power, but also increase our leadership effectiveness, we will have a very strong voice indeed:

1. I always have the ability to choose how I respond to what happens to me. I never have to be a victim.
2. In that space between stimulus and response, I have Three Effective Options.

As they say, leadership is an inside job first. Your ability to know yourself, get clear on what you want to do and be as a leader, check your thinking and your beliefs—all of this contributes to how you are supporting or distracting from the Profit Culture you desire.

KEY POINT

What does Chapter 2 have to do with creating a Profit Culture?

The better you know yourself, the better leader you will be. Leading is being, thinking and doing.

Chapter 3

Gaining Trust
It's Not About Falling
Backwards

Who Cares About Trust?

It's been nothing less than delightful to realize that in the past ten years or so, some bookstore real estate has been devoted not only to the concept of trust at work but also to the methodologies to do something about impacting trust. Certainly, trust came to the forefront when the cover of the *Harvard Business Review* exclaimed in bold letters: **Rebuilding Trust**[12] and inside pages suggested a recommitment to the study of ethics for HBS graduates to come. Once we get the trust thing answered, the rest just seems so much easier.

Trust is not just a nice-to-have, it's a necessary and significant leveraging point in creating a Profit Culture in business. Typically, I define trust a couple of ways:

1. the belief that someone has your best interests at heart.
2. the belief that, for the time being, the other person is going to be honest and up-front; they do what they say they will do (and don't do what they said they wouldn't); they are not going to talk down to you or devalue you.

Sometimes, we use #2 as our definition of "trust at work," because people often will push back and say, "I don't believe that person has my best interests in mind or at heart, therefore I don't trust him," and yet, we can create relationships that work at work where we know someone is going to be truthful, up front and we can work with them, trusting that we can count on them for many things. Even if #2 is the least we can get for trust at work, it's pretty darn good.

---

12   See Roderick M. Kramer's article, "Rethinking Trust," in the June 2009 issue.

Organizational Drag

What happens when organizations suffer from a lack of trust is that they experience Organizational Drag[13]—things that slow them down, get hung up temporarily, or even get stuck for long periods of time. Imagine trying to get your boat to move forward, but you've got the anchor dragging behind hooked on a rock or dug deep in the sand, or you put your foot on the accelerator in your car, only to discover you've left the emergency brake engaged: you're not moving, or if you are, it's with great, strained effort.

What are some of the outcomes you might see when there's a lack of trust at work? Here are some characteristics of Organizational Drag:

- lower performance
- increased interpersonal strife and conflict
- lower productivity
- increased costs
- higher turnover
- higher absenteeism and abuse of vacation or medical leave time
- increased miscommunication
- low team function
- missed goals and deadlines
- decrease in customer satisfaction
- increased grievances and issues escalated to personnel or HR
- missed opportunities for innovation and creativity
- slower time to market with products and services
- poor work quality
- lack of loyalty

Just in case you're wondering how any or each of these might impact your bottom line, look again. Each has, if not an obvious, then a hidden cost that is often difficult to quantify. Just as an exercise, take a look at the above list and see if you can put some numbers to these. What is the estimated annual cost of this condition perpetuated in your organization or on your team?

---

13   Thanks to Ralph Fascitelli from Enthrall Marketing for this!

Lack of Trust or Organizational Drag Costs

Condition	Estimated $ Cost
lower performance	
increased interpersonal strife and conflict	
lower productivity	
increased costs	
higher turnover	
higher absenteeism and abuse of vacation or medical leave time	
increased miscommunication	
low team function	
missed goals and deadlines	
decrease in customer satisfaction	
increased grievances and issues escalated to personnel or HR	
missed opportunities for innovation and creativity	
slower time to market with products and services	
poor work quality	
lack of loyalty	
misuse of technology	
incorrect data or numbers	

It's safe to say that low trust, a lack of trust, or damaged trust costs businesses millions each year, and the craziest thing about this is that much of this loss is largely preventable. Why, then, if it's so blatantly obvious, do businesses persist in thinking that actively cultivating and developing trust is a less worthwhile activity than developing new products or services or hiring new salespeople?

In Real Life

The owner and president of a successful, profitable 18-year old company contacted me because her sales were down by a full one-sixth and she was concerned. During our initial conversation, she had asked me if I could provide sales training or offer new sales techniques to her senior account executives who, for some reason, seemed to have forgotten how to drum up business and close the big sales.

When I met with the group in person, we sat around the table and identified what they believed might be the causes of lower sales—changes in vendor requirements in their industry; more, smaller jobs rather than the big, high-ticket jobs; tougher gatekeeper relationships. Additionally, the president shared that she had recently terminated the sales manager who had worked alongside the team for the past nine years. After a while, I asked the million-dollar question: "what's the trust factor like around here right now?" Dead silence. I tried again: "Well, would you say it's low, medium or high?" Finally, one of the account execs hesitantly offered, "Medium," which was the safest public answer she could give.

Trust was very low indeed. Relationships had been damaged, miscommunication had created upheaval and distress, and there was a huge wall that had emerged between the highest sales producers and the president—nothing was moving forward and everyone had dropped back to protect themselves. What they definitely did not need was sales training or new tools and tricks for closing the deal. Yet, this lack of trust and their inability to deal with it had created a loss of profits and revenue that was increasing by the day!

The Core Dimensions: Behaviors that Create the Foundation, Change the Landscape, and Become the Ballast

Research by scientist Robert Carkhuff in the 1960s identified four core interpersonal behaviors, or helping dimensions, that had a significant impact on those in the helping professions—counselors, therapists, teachers, etc. These behaviors— respect, empathy, specificity and genuineness—were found to be those behaviors that, delivered in high levels, could positively impact a patient relationship. Since that time Carkhuff's research has expansively examined Human Capital Development (HCD) and especially generativity. Eventually, these four initial behaviors grew to include eight in total, including self-disclosure, confrontation, immediacy and concreteness.

In the 1980s, Bob Weyant, a former student of Carkhuff's work, had developed a parenting class where he helped participants utilize the Carkhuff concepts and developed his own models for helping parents influence and confront their children with respect and high-level listening. Eventually, Weyant's work with his own corporate clients led to the key models for communication we use in our Influencing Options® training courses. It's safe to say that this legacy of the core helping dimensions as we use and adapt them is steeped in years of research and thousands of participants from multiple sciences and industries.

The Core Dimensions in The Influencing Option

What do the Core Dimensions have to do with trust? Let's examine each of these four Core Dimensions in the context of a business and see what they have to offer. Much of my work with clients centers around creating cultures that support high levels of trust, productivity, morale, profits and customer delight. They also want to retain their best performers, be seen as an employer of choice, and grow their businesses. If they're non-profits or government agencies, they want the same sorts of things, all the while meeting their mission and purpose.

An environment (relationship, team, business unit, shift, organization) that supports all of the good stuff above, will be an environment where there is consistent delivery of high levels of the Core Dimensions—Respect, Empathy, Specificity and Genuineness. This is more than including these noble concepts on a plaque, poster or listed in your organizational values (as they often are in some form or another). Because *it is our behaviors that influence, not our intentions*, the actual ways you can see these Dimensions in the workplace will determine whether or not you're creating that cultural environment for success. In short, the Core Dimensions—the delivery of high or low levels of such—will impact your Profit Culture significantly.

Respect

When participants in the basic Core Dimensions exercise are asked to come up with behaviors they would observe or experience if they were receiving high levels of **Respect**, their list often looks like this:

- setting a positive tone non-verbally (eye contact, open facial expression)
- active listening
- asking for input/advice
- listening without interruption
- giving credit
- being inclusive
- learning about my culture and preferences
- being courteous and use polite/professional manners
- follow-up and follow-through
- paying attention (no multi-tasking)
- being on time
- showing appreciation
- talking to me as an equal, regardless of position
- neutral/pleasant tone of voice

Using a broader lens, how will you know if your working environment is high in Respect? You might notice these:

- Employees are encouraged to participate in the processes that define how work happens, how it can be improved, and how the organization can prosper.
- Leaders create transparency by communicating clearly, regularly, and using different methodologies, i.e. focus groups, town meetings, newsletter, "what's up" updates, one-on-one conversations, e-mail, etc.
- Individuals are encouraged and supported in developing their talents and strengths
- Values are clearly defined and rewarded and recognized, i.e. you measure success both quantitatively and qualitatively
- Good manners and healthy debate are the norm

Empathy

The second of the four Core Dimensions—Empathy—is often the most misunderstood and perhaps misaligned. A common definition of empathy is "standing in the other person's shoes," and although I'd love to quote Atticus Finch all day, and his advice to daughter Scout in *To Kill a Mockingbird* is legend, the Empathy we develop with our clients is based on specific behaviors that you can develop and decide to replicate.

Here are some behaviors that you might see and/or experience if someone is delivering high levels of Empathy to you:

- Demonstration of understanding via summarizing statements
- Positive non-verbals, including nodding, open body language
- Engagement and presence—no distractions
- Asking clarifying questions or explanations
- Perceiving and naming of feelings
- Showing concern and acceptance, without judgment or agreement

Often, some of my most hard-core business clients cannot see a place for empathy in the workplace. It's about profits, market share and business growth. Or, with law enforcement clients, it's about safety, upholding laws and getting tough on crime. Empathy is for counselors and sissies, right?

Wrong. Empathy—*to demonstrate you understand what someone is feeling and why, without judgment*—is one of the greatest investments you can make in another human being, AND one of the smartest business investments, as well. Sincere and genuine empathy increases trust.

Here's the short version of why:

- if employees trust you, they'll work harder, be willing to give you some wiggle room when you mess up, and they'll support you
- if your customers and clients trust you, they'll want to buy from you even when the price is higher than your competitor
- if colleagues trust you, you'll be better able to collaborate and create win-win scenarios
- if your superiors trust you, you'll be more likely to have increased opportunities for promotion, development and responsibility

It's much easier to demonstrate empathy with someone you like, with someone you respect as a person and someone whose relationship with you is important. It's tougher to demonstrate empathy with people who irritate, annoy or frustrate you, but those are the ones who might need it the most now. The key is this: for the moment, you need to give up your agenda and be utterly and completely engaged and present with the other person. You have to remove your filter of what you think they're saying or that they really mean or what their hidden motives are, and listen very carefully, paying attention to energy and feeling cues, then translate the what and the why without judgment—don't agree or disagree, just let them know you understand. And don't say, "I understand," as your empathy statement because most of the time they won't believe you do until you actually state what you have heard.

Specificity

The third Core Dimension that will help you to create better workplaces, better relationships and better margins on your bottom line is Specificity. I used to say, in public settings, that if I were the kind of girl to get a tattoo on her forehead, it would be "Be Specific," in large, curlicue letters. This always got me strange looks, so I stopped saying it. When I was a writing teacher, I always wished I had a rubber stamp that said "Be Specific!" since it's probably the most frequent marginal note I ever wrote, with the exception of "huh?!"

We are *not* specific enough, which is why we don't often get what we want, or even close to it. Here are some thoughts to consider:

1. **To the degree you are not specific, the person has to guess.** Even if they want to get it right, they want to please you and do what they think you're asking them to do, if you're vague or general, they're going to have to guess and this increases the margin for error dramatically.

2. **Give up the righteous judgment.** I wish I could tell you how many times, when discussing specificity with my clients, someone will say, "well, they're supposed to know this!" or "I pay them a lot of money . . . this is their job!" And so, they don't offer details, specifics or examples, and in the end, they get two-for-one: they get to be right and they don't get what they want!

3. **High specificity and micromanagement are not the same thing.** Sometime in our past, we had a boss, supervisor or leader who micromanaged us, and we hated it. We hate it because it's about a lack of trust, and it's low on all the other Core Dimensions (especially Respect and Empathy). On the other hand, when someone gives us

high Specificity, what it feels like is that the other person is setting us up for success—they are giving us the tools, parameters, outcomes or information that will help us be excellent. That feels nothing like being micromanaged.

What are some of the high-level Specificity behaviors you might see or experience in the workplace?

- Clear and descriptive language
- Provid a graphic or a model, sample or visual aid
- Timelines, timeframes or benchmarks for success
- Check for understanding when giving directions or communicating
- Specific praise or recognition rather than just "good job" or "thanks"
- Processes are clear and precise
- Policies are available and accurate
- Expectations are clear and revisited for updates
- Roles and responsibilities are agreed upon and carried out
- "Success" is clearly defined; everyone knows what the goal is, why, and how they fit into it

Genuineness

The fourth, and final, Core Dimension is Genuineness. Whenever we do the Core Dimensions exercise we often hear that genuineness is something that we can sense—we get a gut feeling that someone is being sincere or truthful with us, but we often have trouble identifying behaviors that demonstrate genuineness explicitly. Genuineness, or authenticity, congruence or even integrity might show up on lists of revered values for organizations, but how do we know either how to deliver it, or that we're getting it? Consider the following:

- consistent behaviors over time, i.e. demonstrated characteristics of honesty or truthfulness
- follow-up and follow-through—their word is good
- focus, engagement, i.e. when they talk or interact with you, they minimize distractions like answering cell phones, computers, etc.
- congruence—what you see is what you get
- no hidden agenda or politics
- demonstrates humility, i.e. owns mistakes, makes amends, apologizes and moves on

As you consider all the Core Dimensions together—Respect, Empathy, Specificity and Genuineness—you can see how when they are delivered together, the affect and impact is exponential. Empathy without Genuineness isn't so effective; Respect without Genuineness feels fake and manipulative.

Manipulation

Speaking of manipulation, often when we help people develop their actual skills in influencing, and especially those types of influencing we want to utilize to positively impact our profit cultures, people wonder if manipulation is faster or necessary. No, and no! First, manipulation does not increase trust, and that's the biggest reason not to engage in it. It seems, in some circles, that there is a fine line between influencing with integrity and manipulation, and yet it's really not all that fine—the biggest differentiator is the delivery of the Core Dimensions themselves. In other words, when we are influencing using the Core Dimensions (more on this in Chapters 6, 7 and 8), we are increasing trust; when we influence using manipulation, we are generally delivering low (or no?) levels of some or all of the Core Dimensions. This is why manipulation doesn't feel good (and decreases trust) to the one who is manipulated. For example, if I convince you to do something (accept my idea, buy my product) and I do so by talking down to you or devaluing you (low levels of Respect), it feels manipulative. Or, if I convince you to do something and later you find out that I did not disclose all of the information that I had (low levels of Specificity), then you feel manipulated by me, and that decreases the trust you have in me. Or, if I am trying to persuade you to do something and I'm not willing to listen or demonstrate understanding (low levels of Empathy) by interacting and answering your questions, you feel manipulated by me. Even if we think it's quicker to manipulate, notwithstanding the ethics factor, the next time we try to influence that person, they remember that we were manipulative last time, and they are resistant and perhaps unwilling to trust us in this interaction. So really, the notion of speed is false if we are talking about an organizational environment where you might want to show up more than one day!

Try this: What Is the Impact of a High/Low Core Dimensions Environment?

Once we clearly define the behaviors that we can see and also replicate in order to increase trust and improve relationships in the workplace, we like to examine how these behaviors are correlative to those conditions we listed at the beginning of this chapter—the potential costs of a low-trust environment.

Reflect for a moment on your own experiences and do the following:

1. Identify someone with whom you currently work or have previously worked who consistently delivered **high levels** of the Core Dimensions to you. In the space below, jot down some descriptors or adjectives that show what it was like to be around that person—what was the impact on you?

2. Conversely, identify someone with whom you currently work or have worked who consistently delivered **low levels** of the Core Dimensions to you. In the space below, jot down descriptors or adjectives that show what it was like to be around this person—what was the impact on you?

When we gather together the lists of descriptors, they are always the same, regardless of the group, the industry, their education levels, their experience, their age, their willingness to participate in such an exercise . . . their answers are *always* the same.

Core Dimensions Impact

High Levels	Low Levels
Trusted	Suspicious
Valued	Frustrated
Encouraged	Stressed
Happy	Tired/Exhausted
Inspired	Angry
Competent	Wary
Confident	Stupid
Safe	Devalued
Supported	Protect myself
Challenged–in a good way	Disappointed
Loyal	Discouraged
Creative	Untrusting
Willing to take risks	Unwilling to do anything extra
Fair	Looking for a new job
Dependable	Unhappy
Respected	

Examine the common list of characteristics for each type of environment—high level or low level Core Dimensions. Column 1 describes the ideal work environment where people are highly engaged, productive, creative and loyal: an environment that supports a Profit Culture. Column 2 describes a dysfunctional or toxic work environment, team or relationship. The only way for a high performer to stay there for any length of time—and they typically don't—is to create their own silo or fortress to protect themselves. The good news is that each type of environment is catching—in other words, you cultivate, by the consistent demonstration of the high or low levels of the Core Dimensions, the exact environment you sow. Not the one you want? Change it up by changing the behaviors. Easy, right?

Reparations: Are Do-overs Possible?

Actually, these concepts *are* simple, but perhaps not always easy, which is why I always have plenty of work to do with my clients. And yet, it demonstrates why having "respect" or "integrity" as core principles or values of your organization is a *good idea*, but doesn't guarantee it will impact your results. Because *it is our behaviors that influence, not our intentions*, if we want to create a Profit Culture, we've got to talk specifically and often about behaviors, and even more than that, we've got to *demonstrate* them. (Talk is cheap!)

What if, you might be wondering, there's some bad blood, history or patterns of miscommunication and dissent? Can we rebuild trust? Are Do-overs possible? Of course! And, they require some specific attention.

This isn't just about being nice

Yet, what we do know is that when we create an environment that fosters high trust, we also get a lot of other good stuff: high productivity, higher morale, better customer service, higher employee retention, higher employee engagement, higher profitability. My clients care about all of those things, and many times they have spent time, energy and resources to try to fix what's not working in their organizations and they want to either ignore the trust factor, or they just don't want to admit the impact it's having on their bottom line, whether it's profits, association membership, meeting their mission, etc. Here's a secret: *if you think it's lack of trust, it probably is.* If you fix a process or a policy and you have people who cannot speak honestly or confront respectfully, you have a nice new process and people who might not follow it. If they are unhappy and morale is low because of lack of trust and fear of dealing with issues, and you give them a raise or change their compensation, you have richer, unhappy people. If you buy a new software program or technology in the hopes that this will streamline your sales process and create access to the data you need, but your team isn't telling you the truth because they don't trust you, you've got another expensive venture into a new technology they're not going to use, and the sales numbers won't go up.

Fixing What's Broken

I've been invited to meet with potential clients who thought their real issues were lack of sales skills, lack of accountability or ownership of issues, low performance, bad hiring practices, or broken processes. Sometimes these are big issues they face, but one of the things we've got to determine initially is whether or not the environment, the trust factor, is an obstacle or a support to success. We know it intuitively, and when pressed, we recognize its symptoms: frustration, suspicion, lack of energy, doing the minimum, gossip or interpersonal strife, negativity, glacially-paced movement. We decide to spend money on expensive team building activities, or taking our groups to the woods, we label ourselves with our personality profiles—I'm a Red J-Driver, You're a Turquoise P-Back-Seater—when really, truly, we need to take a look at trust. You want a culture of trust because *it makes everything easier*. Easier! We accomplish more, we grow faster, we create and innovate, we are inspired; we have more fun. *It's not too good to be true*.

Myths About Rebuilding Trust

Don't be discouraged or fooled by these notions:

Myth #1: It takes a long time. Not necessarily, though it can depend upon the relationship itself and the history among the people involved.

   Presuming Good Intent is a short-cut. In other words, if you can get people together, clearly articulate the goals for increasing trust, define and commit to the behaviors that will increase trust, you can accelerate the process.

Myth #2: It will be uncomfortable. Only if you let it be. Yes, sometimes, we must face either our own (or others) hurt or misgivings, our fear, or our real trepidation about moving forward. No one wants to get burned again and again. Mostly, if you begin the process, what you will feel right away is relief—you are finally working to speak the truth where you haven't before.

Myth #3: Naysayers will sabotage the efforts. What if, in your organization or on your team, this lack of trust has been around for a long, long time? What if it seems like you've had generations of not trusting? Raise the bar! As you lead the efforts to increase trust, you, as the leader, must model the behaviors you want to see, and you must address, immediately, anything that threatens to stifle your movement forward into a more productive, positive work culture with high-performing relationships.

Myth #4: It won't last. Certainly it won't if you don't believe it will! Just as with #3 above, you must carry the flag! Sometimes, you'll need your own mantras, "I am committed to creating and maintaining a positive, productive working relationship with you," or "I want to make sure we're on the same page, so let me make sure I understand where you're coming from." If you've been working to strengthen trust, and something doesn't feel quite right, i.e. communication or relationships seem to be slipping back to old behaviors, address them! Presume good intent, and check it out to see how to get back on track.

Some Truths to Consider: Reality Check

Here are some ideas to keep in mind if your goal is to rebuild trust:

Reality 1: It's easier with leadership commitment. It's true what they say about how the ship is steered—it's easier to have a trust culture when the leaders model those behaviors and when they demonstrate integrity and humility. It is easier, for sure. What if you're not at the top and you are concerned about the lack of trust and the trusting behaviors from the top? You know you've always got three choices: *influence, acceptance and removal!* If you're not sure how to influence "up" effectively, consider both amassing evidence of what a lack of trust is doing to your team or organization, and share those with the other person's self-interest in mind.

Reality 2: The key ingredient is discipline. Changing any sort of long-standing or painful organizational culture element cannot be fixed in a weekend retreat, a team-building activity or a personality profile exercise. It takes real commitment and accountability. You can get a jump-start with some tools or processes, but in reality, you've got to identify the outcomes you want, design a plan to get there, and then commit and recommit. The pay-offs are huge and worth it, but you've got to be *all in*. And get some help if you need it!

Reality 3: Transparency will create transport. Many of my clients, when embarking on changing their cultures to raise the bar and/or navigate real change, recognize that the process might be messy or imperfect. Sometimes, right in the middle, they wonder if it's really going to happen, especially when as the organization begins to turn around, hopes begin to rise, and trust starts to emerge stronger, some element (a person who's not working out or a process that's really tired and ineffective) will become evidently painful. This is part of what happens when we really commit to transparency, truth and a positive movement forward. Step-by-step, day-by-day you will begin to notice a difference and one day, you say, "wow! It feels really different to work here!" or "My relationship with this person has just gotten so much better—it's easier now!"

What does Chapter 3 have to do with building a Profit Culture?

Trust has everything to do with a Profit Culture. No trust? All bets are off.

Chapter 4

Articulating Your Vision: Be specific. Be Specific. Be SPECIFIC.

The purpose of this chapter is to help you get really clear on your vision, identify what your responsibility is in creating and communicating that vision so that your profit culture has a place to go and a destination.

Strategy, Vision, Mission, Plan, Goal: What's the Difference?

Wow—let's string together a bunch of words that have almost totally lost their meaning in business jargon in the past few years! I can see you glazing over right now. We need these concepts defined within the framework of organizational development, so for the purpose of specificity, I'd like to share the definitions I give to my clients so we're clear:

Organizational Development Vocabulary	
Vision	Your best dream of how you want to do business and what impacts/results you want to achieve. Not defined in timelines or what is realistic, at the moment, but is stated as long-range goals and may include: • Services/Products • Resources • Quality • Profitability • Image • Customers/Market • Teamwork/Culture

Organizational Development Vocabulary			
Strategic Profile	Determined by identifying how you want to differentiate yourself in the market—Products, Services, Relationships		
	Competitive	Distinct	Breakthrough
Mission	Your organizational role, charter or assignment; your team's job, products or services it provides to whom. (short and sweet!)		
Values	Your basic core beliefs and values from which all behavior emanates—how you agree to treat each other and your customers.		
Objective/Goal/KPI (Key Performance Indicator)	Specific results or outcomes that you want to achieve; may be time-framed and/or quantifiable		
Short-Term Goals	Time-framed steps that, as they are accomplished, move you closer to your vision		
Action Plan	The specific measurable plan for what needs to occur to achieve a goal, including the who, what, when, how		
Organizational Culture	How people relate to one another—behaviors, communication, norms and processes, formal and informal—moment-to-moment and day-to-day; will be the manifestation of the expected and accepted values.		

The Journey Metaphor

Some time ago, I wrote an article called, "Pick Your Port and Chart Your Course: Yes, you do need a vision!" and I sent it out to my newsletter list. It was full of seafaring references and stories about my father who loves to see everything as a seafaring journey. The journey metaphor can sometimes feel tired, or even cliché perhaps, but frankly, it's a good one. In organizations, we are on a journey together, aren't we? Our destination, summit peak, port of call, or fair city is just a trip away. Our journey may lead to fulfilling our non-profit mission, or enhancing our stakeholder profits, producing excellent goods and services for our customers, providing a public service—the journey fulfills the vision and mission of any organization or group.

In Figure 4.1 you are leading your organization toward the vision and though the path may be wide, everyone is on it. This is an aligned organization.

---

14   Adapted from the work of Alan Weiss.

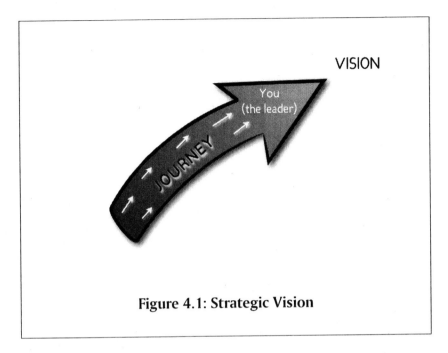

Figure 4.1: Strategic Vision

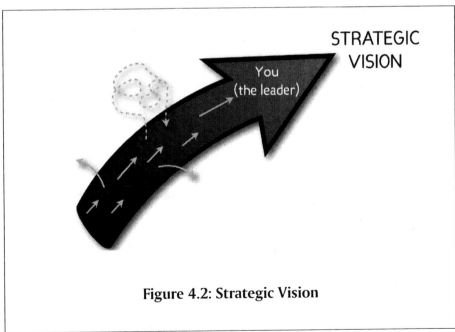

Figure 4.2: Strategic Vision

In Figure 4.2, some have strayed, meandered, or left entirely. This is not an aligned organization. There can be several reasons for a lack of alignment and one important thing for you to do to increase the chances of alignment and everyone moving on the same journey is to clearly articulate your vision.

You are Here

Recently, my parents (now retired) set out on a sailing trip with a few other small sailing craft to explore the islands near British Columbia, Canada, and Vancouver Island. My dad says this is some of the best sailing in the world because there are lovely inlets and coves, tree-filled islands, bald eagles, dolphins and whales, fresh fish and crab to be purchased from the fishers at the docks. In the past, my sister and I complained that when they are on this sort of adventure for weeks at a time, there's no way for us to know where they are in case of emergencies, so this year, my dad, a certified gear-head, was proud to show us a GPS-generating e-mail tool that sent us an update of where they were located about every day or so. We'd get an e-mail from the *Karen Marie* saying, "All is well," with a link to a Google Map. One click and I could see the cove or island where they had anchored or pulled in for the night. *Very cool!*

This is the equivalent of what I like to call the "You Are Here" map that every organization needs—a way to show each individual person, regardless of position or authority—where they are in relation to others in the organization, where their work fits in, and how it helps to fulfill the mission and vision with each task and decision made on a daily basis. Without a sense of knowing how they fit into the big picture, employees do not know how to adjust their inner compass to get on track and in alignment. Without alignment, the best will do their best, and the rest will do . . . *whatever* they do!

I don't think the journey to your ultimate goal has to be as grueling as summiting a mountain peak, we'll utilize the boat metaphor—it works! Also, remember that The Differentiation Factor, introduced in Chapter 1, reminds you that one thing in particular you must do is "clearly articulate your vision and get others to follow," to differentiate yourself as a leader. This chapter is about that identification and clear articulation of your vision. We'll influence others to follow in subsequent chapters.

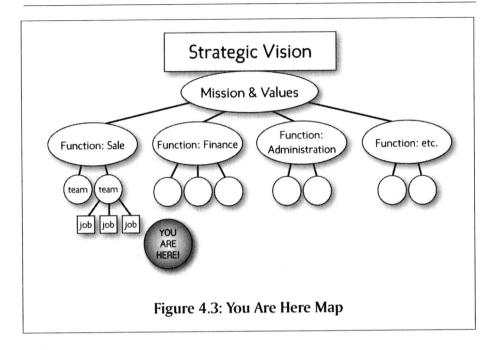

Figure 4.3: You Are Here Map

They Think You Know

If you are at the very top of your company, as an owner or a C-level executive or president, if you are leading a team or business unit inside a large organization, or even if you are leading a small group of individuals toward a destination, they all think you know where you are going. *They think you know.*

In Real Life

Years ago, when I was a college professor near the Olympic Mountain range in Washington, I taught a one-credit hiking class for fun. It was a great excuse to get out and enjoy the magnificent river valleys, the magical Hoh rain forest, the craggy wilderness beaches and pristine alpine meadows. Students would sign up for weekend hikes or backpacking trips and off we'd go in the college van with our gear crammed in the back. The irony of this venture for me is that I have what might possibly be construed as the worst sense of direction on the planet. I've become completely dependent upon my car GPS system, even when I know how to get somewhere! Even though I would repeat many of these hikes over and over in the course of the ten years I was there, I could never remember which hike it was when we climbed bleary-eyed into the van on a misty Saturday morning. I'd have a moment of panic (since I don't even read topo-maps all that well) and ask one of my trusty students, Alan Crawford, if this was the trailhead where we crossed over the river immediately, or the one where the big boulders were piled up on the right? Embarrassing. The group always thought I knew where I was going. They trusted me to have the destination firmly in mind. Luckily, I always had someone with me who was good at this, and luckily, we never got lost. I was supposed to know! Don't be like I was; get your map set and your course charted before you set out!

As an employee, not knowing where you are going has to be one of the top five most frustrating things that can happen in an organization and one of the biggest credibility damagers to a leader. When they think that you don't know where you're going, or that you don't have a clear vision or a clear path mapped out, it's nearly impossible for them to "get on board" with any initiative, goal or series of tasks. Then you start to imagine you've got a bunch of people who are being resistant or difficult, when really, they just can't commit to something they don't understand or clearly see how they fit. Everybody knows this, right? I wish I could tell you that this is a non-issue with most teams or groups, but it's not. It's a big issue! It is your job to clearly articulate the vision.

Helping Them Focus

At one point, I was working with a business owner whose corporation had been successful and profitable for 18 years. When we met, her company was facing some challenging issues internally, as well as a drastic change in her customer base. A very large client, who had represented a third-of their annual revenues for several years, was a major player in the banking decline and was being sold off to another bank. Thousands of people lost their jobs and a big chunk of her business almost dried up overnight. All bets were off.

As we began to take a look at how to rally everyone in the company to look at how they would creatively tackle this pending decline, we began at the beginning—who was she, this company, their clients, and where did she want to go? It was a perfect time to take a really close look and make sure that everyone was truly on-board. The challenge for her at the time was that she felt like everyone already knew what the company mission and vision were because they were working hard in it every day. They were selling and serving their customers, business was happening, so why take time out to state the obvious?

Because, as the leader, it's one of the most important jobs you have—clearly articulate the vision in language that everyone can understand, in a way that engages the hearts and minds of your employees. This, especially, was an important time for her to be the voice for her company—everyone was concerned about losing the major client and worried about job security. They needed to be able to *focus*, and a clear strategy, a clear vision, *helps people focus*.

Getting People "On Board"

One common trap leaders seem to fall into is the "they know this" trap. This is evident when you have a business or group who work for you and because of that fact, you think they know what your vision or mission is, just as the client with the banking customer, above. And, if they think, "we sell stuff" is the vision or "we carry out some this-or-that goal," you're in trouble. Here's why: people, with their engaged minds and hearts, do not board a seafaring vessel for unchartered waters to sell stuff for you. They don't even do it just because you're going to pay them—not for the long term anyway. When we think that pay is the only motivation for our employees and team members to carry out the day-to-day activities of our business, we get ourselves into a pattern of thinking and often behaviors that not only don't support a Profit Culture, they will work against us every time. When, at the writing of this book, it is still estimated that over 60% of the workforce says it is "not fully engaged," there is a lot of room for growth! We line up to get on the boat because we believe one or both of the following:

1. I'm part of something good, great or magnificent by participating in this organization's mission and vision.
2. I'm fulfilling my own personal, professional and soul-ful goals for my own development and my life by being here and participating in this.

This is not to say that salary and benefits aren't important—they are because they are a reflection of the contribution someone is making to the organization's success, their expertise and experience and their talents. When someone's basic needs (aka "survival") are met for their lifestyle choices, the reasons they engage, work hard, stay with you, remain loyal, etc. are not related to money. Still, people leave bosses, not companies, and 75% report each year the reason they leave their job is related to the relationship they have with their immediate supervisor.[15]

In the table below, you can see some examples for a variety of organizations, their core business, and an "on board" idea that can create alignment and buy-in.

Some "On Board" Examples for Vision/Mission

Type of organization	Core Business	"On board" idea
Hospice	End of life care (non-profit)	to respectfully support patients and loved ones as they move through the process of end-of-life transition
Branding and corporate gift company	Creating branded items for events and recognition (for profit/sales)	Helping companies differentiate themselves in the market so that when someone receives a gift or item they are delighted and honored
Correctional Facility	Supervision and housing of convicted offenders (government/civic)	Helping offenders and their loved ones safely navigate incarceration and serving of sentences
Health care equipment call center	Trouble-shooting, dispatch and resolution of equipment issues (for profit/service & sales; global)	Helping hospitals and clinics save lives and maintain a profit margin in their businesses
Office relocation and furniture company	Moving, design, office furniture (for profit/sales & service)	Helping companies to create workplace solutions and spaces they love
Software/firmware development company	Develop and sell high-tech products for businesses (for profit global corporation)	Create simple and effective solutions for business problems

---

15 We discuss this a lot, and what to do about it, in our management and supervisor classes and workshops. However, for our purposes here, it's important to note that no one will get behind a "we want to be a billion dollar company" vision if they don't get 1 and 2, above.

Now, we'll talk about the visioning process as it relates to the Profit Culture you're creating so that you understand how everything fits.

Dream Big

Here's the part where I might get accused of being touchy-feely. I don't care—I get accused of this all the time until people see that what I'm telling them actually gets them results, so they stop calling me that. The very first step in a visioning process is that you've got to give yourself permission to Dream Big.

There are two major challenges with Dreaming Big:

1. **Getting rid of The Negative Voice** that interrupts your process to tell you that you can't have something, it won't happen, the market won't bear it, it's crazy, too progressive, too risky . . . it sounds either like your parent (pick one) angry and lecturing and warning, or a mentor or old boss who thought you had some hare-brained ideas you were trying to pass off as visionary. You must get rid of The Negative Voice. If you can't, at least leave it in the parking lot while you go inside and shop around. The Negative Voice is a crappy dreaming partner. The Positive Voice is the one you want to cultivate and call into the process: this is the voice that says, "what if?" and, "if money were no object . . ." and, "if you could do anything . . ." and prods you on to push beyond your own current thinking and your own current paradigm. This voice is the side-kick to innovation, creativity, and invention. This Positive Voice is your buddy.

2. **Thinking that you have to have a whole bunch of people to help set the vision or strategy**. In the name of good intentions, inclusion and shared governance, this emerges as a big mess for Dreaming Big. Everyone is *not* in on this process, nor should they be. Now, depending on your position and role as a leader, you may have a different focus. If you're at the very top (or an owner), you may have a small group of trusted advisors (your executive team? A small board?) who help with the brainstorming and visioning. Or, if you have a team or a business unit, you may also have this close group. 10 people is too many. 8 people is almost too many. Layers of people in your organization have a role to play in *carrying out* the vision and mission, but they do not set it. This is not to say that you don't do your "research" and listen closely to

ideas through your communication infrastructure, i.e. town meetings, skip-level discussions, surveys, etc. and those *inform* the visioning process, but they do not determine it. *You* set the vision for your scope of responsibility.

Taking time to do the individual, reflective work is essential before you bring in others to brainstorm with you. You've set a creative foundation for your own thinking and participation. What generally happens, however, is that a leader starts to get signs of a rudderless journey or frenetic meandering and thinks, "We should probably do some strategic planning or something," which may or may not result in your desired, intended outcomes. Leaders I know typically do one (or more) of the following:

1. **Nothing**. They're experiencing some kind of success or revenues, so let's not fix what's not broken.

2. **Get a book or go to a class**. They have a sense they should do something, but don't know exactly what, so they embrace a DIY (Do It Yourself) attitude, get a How-To resource and see if they can make it happen.

3. **Put a date on the calendar and put everyone in a room**. Sometimes, they'll facilitate this process with their team themselves, which may or may not produce the results they want, depending on the functioning relationships among the group.

4. **Hire someone to help**. They get a facilitator or a consultant who can help them move through the process of clearly identifying vision and strategy. This generally has one of two outcomes: they spend a lot of money for a cool notebook and a trip to the retreat center in the woods, but they never implement their great ideas fully, or they partner with someone who can help them actually set up the infrastructure to support the strategy and its execution and accountabilities.

Here's a clean map of a suggested path to creating a process that yields real results, and supports the sustainability of a profit culture:

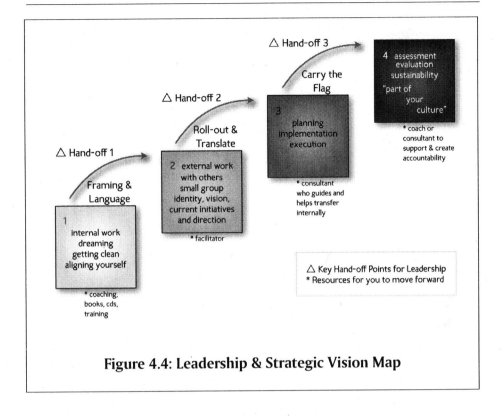

Figure 4.4: Leadership & Strategic Vision Map

Three Critical Factors: Hand-offs for Your Clear Articulation

Notice the "hand-off" points on Figure 4.4: Framing and Language, Roll-out and Translate, and Carry the Flag. These are critical for you as a leader. The handoff is how you, as a leader, help craft the transition to the next step in the process of rolling out and executing your Strategic Vision.

1. Framing and Language

Many a great vision died in someone's head. People who are noted visionaries and who decide to lead others must be able to get their brilliant ideas out of the creative, thinking parts of the brain and into articulated language. There are lots of ways to do this: writing, talking, or a combination thereof, but the point is you must be able to use language to convey. This is not only important in the first hand-off, but also throughout. Your language use, your choice of words, your use of your voice (Chapter 2) is essential here to differentiate you as a leader and to help gain clarity for yourself and your organization. If you're not good at this, get a coach or mentor. Don't waste time, or muddle through, get someone to help you and be the objective listener so that you can learn to check yourself for clarity and understanding. Language differentiates everything and every leader. As my mentor says: the person who controls the language, controls the situation, controls the relationship, controls the sale—and we're not talking about *being* controlling, we're talking about steering the ship. You must improve your language skills consistently to remain effective.

2. Roll-out and Translate

You, and your team of executives or other top leaders in the organization, create the message for the roll-out of the vision and the strategy. If you are a middle manager, translation of the strategy and vision is your job most of the time. This is the part where you help people really see themselves in the big picture, this is the "you are here" moment and it's important because you want to proactively remove any obstacles to buy-in, commitment, or getting on board. Often, creating buy-in and commitment for a vision or goal is one of the most crucial interchanges you can manage as a leader. It's one of the two strongest elements for creating a foundation for better influencing, for the long term, and helps to gain trust and credibility. Often, when it's a new strategy or vision (during a roll-out) we are also trying to manage change, and you must deal with the issues that arise around change: fear, anxiety, misunderstandings or potential obstacles.

3. Carry the Flag

This should be the easiest part—to continually enforce and reinforce movement toward the vision and fulfillment of the strategy—because you, as the leader, were the one who came up with this vision in the first place, right? Or at least you had a part in it and developed your own initial buy-in for the vision. It's not the easiest part, although it might be the most simple. It's not easy because the gravitational pull in organizations is away from the strategic vision and into the weeds— into the fire-fighting and the reactive mucking about in the operational details. When you shift your focus from the big vision, and you drift from it, your group follows. Instead, you need to create a discipline of regularly messaging and framing decisions, initiatives and task in light of how they are contributing to the overall goals and vision.

As Verne Harnish says in *Mastering the Rockefeller Habits*, it doesn't matter if everyone starts mocking you, reciting the mission or vision statements—in fact that's a sign that they are internalizing the message and that helps them align themselves with that big vision.

In Real Life

I called to check in with a company president who had been a client the previous year. She had done a lot of work with her organization and team, especially around clarifying vision, mission and values. We had also created a workable performance management system so that her employees had regularly scheduled one-on-ones to proactively manage any performance issues and to give regular praise and feedback. She had reported a significant, positive change in work atmosphere, productivity and performance. Their profits were increasing.

During our call, however, she expressed some dismay at a recent team meeting where one of her most vocal employees posed the question, "can you tell us a little about the direction the company is going?"

"Didn't I just spend all last year addressing this?" she exclaimed to me. "How many times do I have to repeat myself?"

"Over and over and over," was my reply, and it still is. You enforce the vision; you carry the flag.

Carrying the flag means that you are the one who is responsible for the message, over and over. Don't get caught in the trap that you think you told people about your vision, and their parts in it, one time after you had your "strategic planning" meeting and you are assuming everyone gets it, is on track and will stay on track. The pull of the every day operational issues can steer people off-track very quickly. On the other hand, a clearly articulated vision helps your team focus on what's important and gives them a compass by which to navigate their daily decisions and tasks.

Compass Questions

Once you've clarified the vision and mission, below are some questions that can help with focusing and aligning your people with the vision and mission. Imagine that, at each question or decision point, your team members could use these Compass Questions.

1. How does this contribute to the success of my organization?
2. How does this impact my ability to contribute to fulfilling the mission or vision of my organization?
3. How will the outcome of this create a win-win and uphold our organizational values?
4. What if I don't do this?

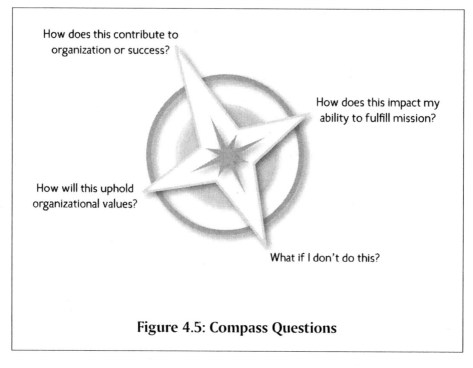

Figure 4.5: Compass Questions

Specificity

In Chapters 3 and 6, we spend a lot of time discussing the merits and significance of Specificity; however, in particular, when you are clearly articulating your vision, your Specificity is key, especially when you are answering the "you are here" questions, helping people to see alignment among their jobs, their aspirations, and your organization's success. You help connect the dots with Specificity. For a while, we had a coffee mug we offered as gifts to clients that said, "In the Spirit of Specificity, Tell Me What You Want!" and it was one of the most popular items we had.

We all get a great sense of relief when we are alleviated from having to read someone's mind, and as the leader it is your job to help people make those connections to buy-in and commit to the vision and mission.

A Word about Infrastructure: Communication and Performance Management

In their 2002 book, *Execution: The Discipline of Getting Things Done*, authors Larry Bossidy and Ram Charan suggest that two of the primary reasons that great strategies never get off the ground are the lack of emotional fortitude of the leader and no infrastructure to support things actually happening. In my work, emotional fortitude is developed through practices that involve self-reflection, self-assessment and self-development through practice and skills. Self-confidence and self-esteem are highly significant, as well. When I described the Differentiation Factor[16], the confronting element is directly related to emotional fortitude. It takes strength and courage to address issues or problems in a respectful, direct manner and not let things go on so long that they erode the good work or good relationships of an organization.

The infrastructure necessary in an organization to carry out a great vision and/or strategy involves two primary elements outside of specific business processes (i.e. manufacturing protocol or work flow standards). The first element is **communication**, especially as it relates to the dissemination of information, the gathering of feedback, the ability to assess and evaluate successes and failures, and specific skill sets around communicating, influencing, resolving conflict, problem solving and decision-making. Many of the skills and tools outlined in this book help organizations create that infrastructure and expertise for communicating. Additionally, the second important element in your infrastructure is a **performance management**[17] system that helps employees clearly see their roles, responsibilities and results clearly articulated for them. Managing performance is part of the fulfillment of the vision and important individual maps that will help people chart their courses for success. This is about proactively managing performance on an ongoing basis[18].

---

16   Differentiation Factor: the ability to clearly articulate a vision and get others to follow AND confront issues quickly, directly and respectfully.

17   A little more about Performance Management in Chapter 10.

18   See http://www.libbywagner.com/articles/special-reports.php for a free Special Report on Performance Management for the Six Keys to Managing Performance.

What does Chapter 4 have to do with building a Profit Culture?

You don't want a rudderless, absent-captain ship: you need a vision so you can get out of the harbor and know where you're headed!

Chapter 5

On the Same Page: Influencing Commitment on a Team

Team Building

To imagine how much time, money and energy are spent each year, around the world, on "team building" is mind-boggling. I tried to come up with some rudimentary numbers and it's into the billions. What is it, exactly, that people are trying to do as they make this investment in teams? The collaborative approach to getting things done is not new, for sure, and organizations call for the dynamic of the team to become a major vehicle for reaching their objectives.

Team building exercises, methodologies and philosophies seem infinite. Here are some I've seen, participated in, or heard of:

- Taking some type of personality indicator or assessment (i.e. Myers-Briggs®, DiSC®) and interacting around it
- Experiential learning, i.e. ropes courses, challenge courses, geo-teaming
- Kinetic activities, i.e. building Legos®, PVC pipe construction, toothpicks and marshmallows architecture
- Games, i.e. Bingo, Jeopardy, Monopoly
- Some sort of "fun" outing, i.e. boat cruise, bowling, golfing, amusement park, river rafting, ball game
- Sharing in a charitable or volunteering activity together

Admittedly, some of these sound interesting or even fun, right? Yet for some, the mere mention of *any* of these creates an urge to run in the other direction. Come on! What about fun? Shouldn't teams who have fun together be able to work together better? Not necessarily.

I'm not opposed to fun, and I'm not even going to tell you that any of these are a bad idea in general, but they won't get you a great team and they won't create any increased commitment to your building a Profit Culture. What they can do, if done well, is enhance a team's interactions, create memories, and perhaps camaraderie. Many of them, especially the experiential, when facilitated by an talented facilitator, can create common language, metaphor and symbolism for the team culture you may desire. If a group has challenges building a PVC pipe construction because they don't communicate well or can't take direction or problem-solve, it's probably a decent indicator that that communication dynamic can exist in their real working interactions. But the *real* work of building teams comes in creating *real* work projects where they have to interact, collaborate, resolve issues, get real results, be accountable for their outcomes, and become interdependent.

Team or Committee?

One of the first things you need to determine is whether you have a team or a committee. There are reasons for both. The biggest difference is that teams cannot win—get the desired results or reach the goal—without each other. Committees, which may be gathered together, can each fulfill their responsibility or part and reach the goal without someone else relying on them. Thus, the committee can achieve results, but it is not interdependent. So, our definition of a team, for the sake of this discussion, is this: groups of people gathered together to fulfill a particular purpose or goal and on which the members are interdependent. In other words, the success of the team depends upon their ability to utilize the specific talents and skills of each member and the goals of the team cannot truly be reached without their relying upon one another to do his or her part. Committees, on the other hand, may indeed be collections of individuals gathered for a common purpose, i.e. to approve a budget, or outline a project, but they represent individual interests and perhaps see themselves as spokespersons for the interests themselves, such as in a council meeting.

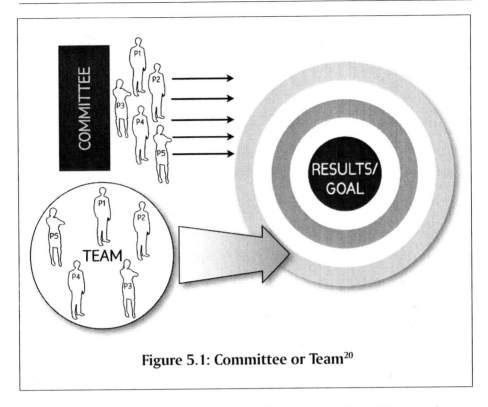

Figure 5.1: Committee or Team[20]

If you want your group of people to behave like a team, and you'd like to influence them as a team, then you need to make sure they've got the infrastructure to do just that. In our work, we've found the following elements helpful in setting up strong teams for Profit Cultures:

1. Clarify the goal/results of the team itself
2. Check for alignment
3. Create a Team Agreement
4. Clear the Swamp
5. Create Action and Accountability

Clarify the Goal

As discussed in Chapter 4, it is essential in your leadership and in your influencing effectiveness to have a clearly articulated vision. Any team different from the executive team of an organization has a sort of "sub" vision that contributes to the overall mission/vision of the organization. Your team needs to know their goal on

---

20   Adapted from Alan Weiss' *The Son of Process Visuals*, 2007.

several levels, but especially the *what*. What is it they are responsible for achieving in their work together? What are the desired results? What are the outcomes of their work as a team? Individual members no doubt have specific responsibilities and tasks, but the sum total of the responsibilities, tasks, tactics, etc. must lead to something clear. Before you can influence them to go there, to work together to do so, you need to paint a clear picture of exactly what that is.

The Importance of Alignment

Once we know what the goal is, we need to check for alignment. Experts on multi-generational workforce issues suggest that one of the ways to get people of different generations, with varying values and relationships to their work, to work together effectively on teams is to create alignment among the goals of the organization, goals of the team itself and the goals of the individuals. If the individual can clearly see that to work toward meeting the team goals is to help himself and the team can see that to work toward the organizational goals is to help the team—you have alignment. Often, it is the job of the leader to help individuals and teams see this alignment and create a way to appeal to the self-interest of the individuals who make up the team.[21]

What is Your Team Responsible For Achieving?

There are two ultimate responsibilities of your team—to meet the technical, specific goals you've set for them, i.e. sales numbers, customer service standards, work quality *and* to maintain a healthy environment in which to work. Normally, when we begin to pay attention to managing the performance of our employees, we examine these two elements—technical skill and interpersonal skill—and we set expectations for that person's job duties and responsibilities. Normally, even in the worst situations (worst = there are no specific job standard expectations or outcomes), most have an understanding about the technical responsibilities of their work. Unfortunately, so many times, *organizations neglect to be specific about what the expectations are for how they will behave around one another* because they imagine that they have hired people who will know how to focus on their work, communicate effectively and solve problems efficiently. This is not to say that you expect that your team members are "damaged" and cannot do this well, but just as if you let someone approach the task of a new job and did not offer training or

---

21   See Figure 4.3: You Are Here in Chapter 4.

specifications about what a good job looks like, *you'd get what you get.* If you want to create a strong corporate culture of communication and respect; if you want to infuse interactions with the Core Dimensions not only because it's the right thing to do but because it creates a Profit Culture, then you need to be specific about what interpersonal behaviors are expected on your team.

Creating a Team Agreement

For our clients, creating a Team Agreement is one of the most effective, most powerful processes we do. It just sounds so simple, so obvious, that it's almost easily dismissed as unimportant, but let me assure you, it is not. Just a quick visit to www.libbywagner.com/about/testimonials you can read many examples of how a leader cites the dramatic effect their own Team Agreement[22] had on the outcomes of a project or on their workplace in general. This is a big deal.

Here is the outline of the Team Agreement creation process[23]:

1. **Identify and clarify the specific Results, Goals, etc.** that allow this team to fulfill the organization's mission/vision. You need to do this beforehand so you can clearly articulate the outcomes or goals for them. I like to use chart paper or a poster that has the specifics on it so we can visually see it while we complete the other steps.

2. **Clarify (with the group) the characteristics of the ideal "dream" team,** i.e. a GREAT Team. You will have some of these characteristics already, but there will be some that you won't demonstrate consistently. At first, this may seem silly, but it's really important. Everyone knows what a GREAT team is and I encourage them to think about it beyond the scope of the workplace: sports, community activities, etc. We create a big poster of characteristics and fill up the page so that we've got a picture of the "dream" qualities.

---

22   I've included a few sample Team Agreements in the appendix so that you can see how simple they are, and how powerful they can be for a group.

23   Visit www.libbywagner.com for a free article on Team Agreements and a webinar recording of a more detailed walk through the process.

Figure 5.2: Team Agreement

3. **Put the GREAT Team poster next to the Results/Goals poster and ask this question**: "If our team is going to being a GREAT team and get the results we want to fulfill the mission/vision of the organization . . . what would we need to be willing to do together?"

4. Depending on the size of the group, you may want to do the next part together as a whole, or split up into smaller groups to generate more ideas. **Identify 5-7 things (actions/behaviors) that the group**

says are indicative of what the team values, believes, etc. about their interactions with each other, your customers or clientele, and others in the organization. No doubt, you will come up with some common themes and the facilitator's job is to make sure that once you identify your 5-7, you must define them behaviorally: in other words, you ask, "what would that look like?" or "how would someone know that was important to us?" You can check this out in the examples in the Appendix.

5. **Finesse the language so that it says what you want simply and succinctly.** It has to sound like the group, and you want it to have minimal jargon or acronyms.

6. **Gain agreement and commitment.** Have everyone sign it, if you want. At the top of all the ones we do, we write, "We promise to do our best to . . . " Some teams make foam board posters and have them where people can see them. Others frame them and everyone gets a copy. Some create laminated versions or wallet cards.

7. **Carry the flag!** Now the Team Agreement becomes part of your team culture and organizing principles. Integration is the second-most critical piece of this process—if you don't carry the flag, two potential outcomes may occur: your exercise will be for naught and/or your credibility will be diminished because you made them engage in an exercise and there was no real change or follow-through.

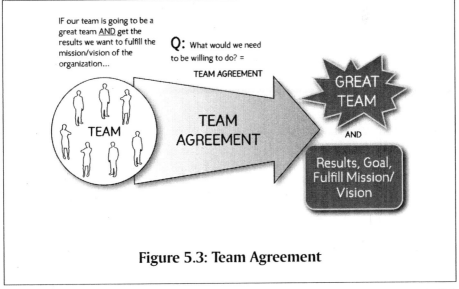

Figure 5.3: Team Agreement

Seriously, that's it. You can do it in less than 2 hours[24], especially if you're good and you can keep people on-track!

Removing Obstacles to Motivation

What if you've got this team, and they seem to be pretty good, they've even got a working Team Agreement and yet, something's not working smoothly. Sometimes their performance is inconsistent, or they don't always meet their goals (or if they do it seems at great cost), or they seem to get hung up on "history" and old, bad stuff that has created baggage or interpersonal strife. How can you motivate them? How can you inspire them to get to the next level, move on, or move closer to that Profit Culture we desire? Do we need to go back to the list at the beginning of the chapter and take everyone bowling? Hire an inspirational speaker and have a retreat?

This is a really critical point because so many leaders, with good intentions, get the sense that something's in the way of having this super, high-performing team and they want a special pill or silver bullet to fix what seems to be broken. Then they get this idea that perhaps because of all the change and the increased workload and the demands on everyone's time, the team just needs a little inspiration. They just need a stress reliever and maybe a dose of motivation.

You cannot motivate anyone. This is counter to what many will tell you is your job as a leader—you may have been taught that you must motivate, control or cajole, perhaps even inspire others to do what you want them to do—the work they are paid to do and that you are paid to oversee. You're not. And you cannot. Motivation comes from within, and for the most part, individuals choose what motivates them and what de-motivates them. I will say that we often confuse the terms *motivate* and *inspire*, and I see them as distinct. I can, as a leader, inspire others to follow or to emulate me by modeling my actions and behaviors, by *leading from the front*. Perhaps they can feel motivated by this quality of my leadership, but ultimately, they choose to move or not, to follow or not, to change or not. This is why, in terms of influencing and leading a Profit Culture you'd be better served to identify your team's perceived de-motivators and deal with them directly and specifically to clear the way for them to motivate themselves. You need to Clear the Swamp.

24　Sometimes, we do this as part of a whole team development process day or retreat, but you really can do it in 2 hours or less. If your team is really struggling, dysfunctional, or has really low trust, there's some pre-work you need to do to facilitate this, or get someone to help you so it doesn't backfire. You can also call me: 206-906-9203 and I'll be happy to answer some questions.

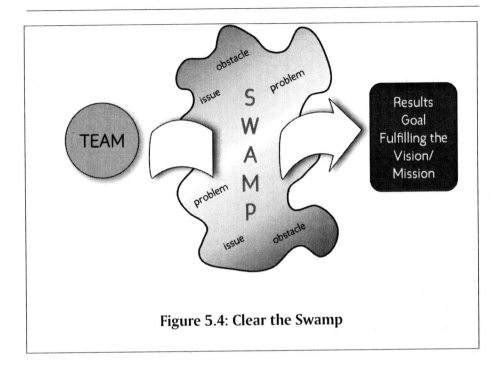

Figure 5.4: Clear the Swamp

Clearing the Swamp

Clear the Swamp is another process we use in team development to help teams identify, assess and deal with issues and obstacles in the way of high performance. It's another really simple tool that you can facilitate (or have someone else) to move your team consistently, smoothly forward toward the results and goals you've set for them. There are three "golden rules" for swamp clearing that are important to note before you begin:

Rule 1: You, as the leader, should be part of the process in some way. You can facilitate it, but sometimes it's better for you and the team if someone else facilitates. You'll probably know, once you read the entire process, how your dynamic might impact this process. Either way is fine, but typically, you should be part of the process.[25]

Rule 2: If you're going to Clear the Swamp, it can't be a one-time thing. You need to make a minimum commitment to a particular timeframe, such as six months, two quarters, or a year. Much like with the Team Agreement, if you make people

---

25   As soon as I start making up rules, I have to talk about when you can break them. If your team is really, really struggling, i.e. low trust, dysfunctional behaviors, etc. and you have doubts whether they would participate openly and honestly with you in the room, there are alternate ways to gather the data.

go through an exercise and there's no follow-through or change, they disengage further and your credibility is damaged. Clear the Swamp, especially, creates hope, and when we do set the expectations that we're moving toward positive change, and then don't follow-through, that also can damage trust and commitment. Do it right, or don't do it at all.

Rule 3: Be prepared to respond and don't get defensive. Chances are you, your leadership behaviors and style, are going to come up and/or come into question. It's a normal part of the process. The important thing to remember is that we are dealing with perception, which at the time, is someone's reality. You need to respond openly and courageously, but this is about the team identifying what it perceives as the greatest obstacles it currently has to success. You could be one, and that's important to know, too.

Facilitating the Process

Set Up: The easiest way to begin is to envision figure 5.4 and to have, either on a poster or white board or some equivalent, the language that describes the Results/Goals that this team is called to do to fulfill the Mission/Vision of the organization. If you've done the GREAT teams exercise, that's a good one to put along side the Results/Goals because those both represent where you want this team to consistently and persistently go—towards the goal!

Step 1: Gathering the Data

Pose one of the following questions to your group (see below for options for different kinds of team dynamics[26]):

1. "Right now, what do you see standing in the way of our having a GREAT team and meeting these goals/results?"
2. or, "What's an obstacle or issue preventing us from moving to the next level for our team?"
3. or, "What are the issues and obstacles or problems preventing us from having high levels of productivity, trust and morale?"

Any of these questions can work; you choose based on what you have identified as the results/goals you are moving toward.

---

26   If your team has a high level of trust, you can do this first process of gathering data in a group set-ting together. If not, you may want to gather perceived obstacles/issues via an anonymous survey or one-on-one interviews. Either way, you are first simply gathering information so that you can address specific issues/obstacles.

It's important at this stage in the process that you try not to censor their answers. Depending on how you're gathering the information—in the larger group, one-on-one or anonymously—you may hear repetitions or perhaps even some issues that arise that are bothersome. Typically, the bothersome items come in two forms: they're about you or they're about someone else specifically in the group. Know that this process takes courage, like all of those outlined in this book, and if your team tells you that *you* are the biggest problem standing in the way of their success as a team, you can examine that feedback for validity and make decisions about how to move on. It's unwise either to take this type of feedback as absolutely true or absolutely false. It's most likely in between and it's your job to find out why.

Any time I've worked with a team, and especially those teams that are not doing so well, I let the leader know[27] that there is a good chance that they will want to blame their failures or supposed inabilities on the leader. I suggest that he be prepared for this and be prepared to respond as appropriate. Generally, issues that are de-motivating to your team that are related to you may not show up in the process discussion as, "our leader," but instead couched in issues such as, "communication," or, "no recognition," or "management doesn't listen to our concerns." The important thing to remember at this point, and this is critical, is that while you are gathering their perceived obstacles or de-motivators, do not judge, just gather. This is a way to listen, as when demonstrating empathy, that you have understood and heard—you are not agreeing or disagreeing at this point in the process.

Step 2: Recording

Depending on how you've gathered your data, you will want to assemble the list for all to see in a group meeting. If you've done it right there, you've got a chart or board with the items listed if you've gathered them beforehand, you've got a chart or board prepared before the session. You want to list the issues or obstacles on the left-hand side along with two other columns left blank with the following headings.

Your chart should look something like this:

Issue or Obstacle	Can we influence it?	Is it worth it?

27   See Golden Rule #3.

Fill in the issues in column 1 you have gathered from your team members. Once, I facilitated a group who filled up a floor-to-ceiling whiteboard with issues! It doesn't matter how many you have because most likely many are interrelated. Press them by saying, "anything else?" and by asking for Specificity to clarify. When things start getting repetitive, they're finished.

Step 3 Assessing

Next, you'll want to make your way down the list with some *minimal* discussion of each item. The reason you want it to be minimal is that at this time you are going to qualify those issues that the team (or you) can actually do something about, i.e. influence, and whether or not it's worth it to try to do so. You are leading them through a process of not only prioritizing but also validating.

Take a look at the following chart:

Swamp Chart (sample)

Issue or Obstacle	Can we influence it?	Is it worth it?
1. Communication to upper management		
2. Budget cuts for equipment		
3. Getting completed projects from other teams		

Taking your team through this beginning list (and these are often common obstacles or issues that come up),might go something like this:

For Number 1, You say: "If communication to upper management is an issue that's preventing us from meeting our goals successfully, is this something we can try to influence?" They may say "yes" or "no" and you will want to guide that discussion. Chances are that they, often with your help, can try to influence this and importantly, as the third column suggests, it's worth it to them. That means, this item stays on the current list, and you put a "Y" in column 2 and a "Y" in column 3.

For Number 2, You say, "If budget cuts for equipment is an issue that's preventing us from having high levels of productivity, trust and morale, is this something we can influence?" Your situation will dictate this answer depending on where you are in your budget cycle, whether requests of this type are being accepted, etc. However, for the sake of this illustration, let's say the answer is "No. We cannot currently influence the budget in order to get new equipment."

This next point is critical in the swamp clearing process because your group, in agreement, has identified an obstacle *that they cannot currently influence*, which means it is causing some distraction for them that they can do nothing about. This is where you might say:

> *"If we're in agreement that this is the current situation, then my expectation is that for now, until the situation changes, we are not going to spend any more time being distracted by it, and in fact, we're going to think of creative ways to get around it."*

Or something like that. The point is that you *cross it off the list* for now, in front of the group, and you ask for their willingness to commit to a common action or practice. Either, you request that they stop moaning and groaning about this issue, which distracts them from other, productive behaviors, or you identify a way that they can prepare for the next opportunity in a budgetary cycle. Your situation, again, will dictate the appropriate response, but the important thing is that the group agrees *to let it go for now* since it cannot be changed. This is very powerful and re-focuses them on those things that are within their power to influence.

You make your way through the entire list assessing each one. You will find that most (almost all, actually) of the issues are actually influence-able. Sometimes, it would require action by you, the leader, and other times the team members themselves would need to do something. Sometimes, because of timing or other priorities, it's not worth it. What's important is that as a group, together, they are examining their own de-motivators, assessing their ability to do something about them, and the next step will help you and the group move on.

Step 4: Prioritizing and Selecting

Sometimes, for this next part, I get those sticky dots and give people each two of them. We line up the poster(s) and give them a break and ask them to identify what they believe to be the top 2 priorities for this team. In other words, if we could solve/resolve this issue, we'd get the most "bang for our buck" and make some real progress moving forward. They may resist a little because they will have more than 2 that they want, but keep them to 2 because it's likely, for the group, that you will actually identify a Top Three list if the voting is close.

Once everyone has voted, identify the team's top 2 or 3 issues/obstacles. These will be the current priorities for this team to work on to develop and improve (or get to the next level, etc.). One thing that's important to do here is to tell them that the other things on the list are not going away—they remain on the list until the group says they are no longer obstacles. This is another reason why you can't do this process only once—you have given them your word that you will come back to this, and you need to do that. How long? It depends. Some teams Clear the Swamp once a quarter or twice a year. Once a year would be a minimum if you've got otherwise good communication and interactions. Longer than that is too long.

Step 5: Discussion and Action Steps

Depending upon the size of your team, you may want to split into smaller groups, i.e. two or three groups, depending upon the number of issues that ended up a priority. Each small group should do the following:

A. Perform a simple gap analysis:
1. What's the current state of this issue? What's going on that's not working?
2. What's the desired state of this issue? What would it look like if it was working well or corrected or thriving?
3. What are some recommendations we have for resolving this? (2-3)
4. What is the first, next step for each recommendation?

B. Report out to the larger group.

Here, your role as the leader is to pay attention and delegate appropriately. Consider the recommendations they are making, and if you need more time to evaluate them—you do not have to do it on the spot—say so and then make sure you do respond at an agreed-upon time. Remember, we do Clear the Swamp for two reasons: to identify and remove obstacles to motivation *and* to create a stronger, more resilient, more committed team. Actively participating in a fruitful Clear the Swamp process may not be as fun as bowling or jumping off of a 30-foot Power Pole, but the long-term impact on your team and its ability to get stronger and produce greater results is significant. Everyone wins.

Creating Action and Accountability

Whether it's staying true to your Team Agreement or following up on action you've identified as important outcomes of the Clear the Swamp process, you want to be able to set people up for success by helping them create a behavioral commitment to these agreements made in the moment. Again, much of this involves your "carrying the flag" again—how can you take these processes, their outcomes and insights and weave them into the ordinary work, the benchmarks and check in points.

Some groups utilize the Team Agreement as an important tool for discussion around performance. In other words, the person is not only responsible for their technical performance expectations, KPIs (Key Performance Indicators) or competencies,[28] but also for the behavioral agreements you've committed to in your Team Agreement. Recently, we've used a survey tool to have teams evaluate themselves and each other on how well they are demonstrating what they said was important to them (approximately 6-12 months after original agreement creation). It's a great exercise in examining one's own perception versus the perception of others on the team, and allows for a fruitful discussion, readjustment of goals, or a recommitment to some of the Team Agreement behaviors that have been slipping over time.

Creating accountability around the Clear the Swamp process really involves delegating the prioritized issues the group selected and creating some action steps, timelines and desired outcomes around them. It's important for two reasons:

1. They identified these obstacles, they agreed they could influence them, and they assessed their importance. That allows for ownership, so give it to them! Ensure that the team follows up—it's empowering to do so.
2. You don't need to take on the work that your team needs to be doing. Delegate, empower, back off, and check in when appropriate.

Additionally, you have to be accountable for revisiting the Clear the Swamp process after an appropriate amount of time, as suggested before, such as in three months or six months. When you revisit, reassess, and check progress, it creates a way to praise efforts being made, check in to see what might need to be readjusted, and creates that sense of team and empowerment that we want to foster. It also allows you, as a group, to identify things that are not on the list anymore—they are no longer issues or obstacles, and that's good news! Additionally, if something new has emerged, you can address it right away rather than letting it fester. This really helps to support and sustain the Profit Culture you are building. Remember, the worst thing you can do is make them go through the process and never go back to it.

---

28   All of these terms are performance system lingo, and what it really means is the results or outcomes that person is technically responsible for carrying out in his or her job.

What does Chapter 5 have to do with building a Profit Culture?

There's simply nothing more powerful than a highly dynamic, resilient, creative team. You want to use your resources and actions wisely to really build your team rather than just going through the motions of "team building."

Chapter 6

"By That I Mean . . ."
Asking for What You Want

A common initial client visit when we are discussing how to create Profit Cultures might go like this:

Me: *What's currently going on that you are interested in addressing or about which you have concerns?*

Client: *Well, my VP of sales doesn't seem to be holding his people accountable for the numbers we projected at the beginning of the year.*

Me: *What do you think the issues are?*

Client: *The market is down, seems like our customers just aren't buying.*

Me: *What is your VP currently doing to address these obstacles with his team?*

Client: *He has regular sales meetings, sometimes goes out on calls with the team . . . calls them on the carpet when they don't get their numbers.*

Me: *What do you want the VP to do?*

Client: *I want him to do his job—bring in sales via his team!*

Me: *Do you think he knows exactly what you want?*

Client: *I don't think you understand! I pay him a lot of money to be in this position . . . I shouldn't have to babysit a VP of sales to bring in sales—that's what I pay him to do!*

> **Me**: *Yes, that is what you pay him to do. Let's take another look. What have you done already to communicate to him that he needs to improve his performance as the VP?*

> **Client**: *I don't know how much more clear I can make it—we look at the sales numbers every week!*

And so on.

Now, I do not assume anything about this client, or any of my clients, and I especially do not assume that he's damaged, stupid or ignorant. However, I do pay close attention to the language that people use when they share what's going on and what they'd like to change. Chances are, in this situation, and in many like it, this CEO *hasn't really asked for what he wants.* He may be making a couple of common errors:

1. He's focusing on what he doesn't want—the low sales or the low performance.

2. He's lacking detail or specifics in both identifying what he wants and what he doesn't want.

Let's examine each and discuss why it's important to do so when you are working to create a great environment for profits. First, I have no idea why we do this, but we often focus on what we don't want—the undesirable behaviors or characteristics—and we do so because it's then that we notice there's something we don't like that needs to be changed. I do think this is necessary. We need the contrast. We need to say to ourselves, "well, I don't like *that*!" so that we can assess the situation, make decisions about choosing some other tack, or move into problem solving to deal with the issue. What happens often is that when this involves someone else, we get sort of stuck there, describing what we don't like and what we don't want. This often comes out in the form of a confrontation, conflict or even argument. We "call someone on the carpet" or we have a "come-to-Jesus talk" or we "read them the riot act." We tell them *exactly* what we don't like and we don't mince words.

Generally, even after this, we don't get what we want. And if we do, because the person is motivated by fear or the pain or discomfort of this interaction, it never lasts for long. The results are short-lived for the same reasons that an overuse of Position Power creates that short-term compliance rather than the long-term commitment that we want. Often, I share the example of telling a child, "Don't slam the door!" What we really want is for the child to close the door quietly behind him as he comes in, but that's actually *not* what we asked for, and because the brain has no way of seeing the concept of "don't," we typically get the slammed door every time. It's a simple, yet powerful distinction.

Second, lack of Specificity is just a big waste of time all around. Certainly the most common error here is to be vague, expecting the person to just get it, or read your mind, or worse, you get really righteous about how they *should* know what you're talking about: they've been on this job for a long time, you're paying them lots of money, they're grown-ups, credentialed . . . you get the picture? So, we leave out details and specifics about what we want because we think they should already know. Sometimes, with our best intentions, we think we'll offend or be perceived as talking down to someone if we get specific about what we want. In reality, high Specificity, along with the other Core Dimensions (Respect, Empathy and Genuineness) helps the person clearly understand what we want, what's expected, and generally they're happy not to have to do the extra work of guessing or mind reading!

When I encounter a conversation with a leader, such as the one listed above, fairly soon in the conversation, I will say, "did you ask for that?" And most of the time, the response is either, "no," or "they should know already," or a combination of both. Certainly, we've all experienced the frustration of a communication situation where you feel like this person should just know what you mean, or you've discussed it before . . . and yet, the only real result that comes from this kind of righteous disappointment is that you get to be right . . . and you don't get any closer to getting what you want.

You, as translator

One of the most distinctive characteristics of a good influencer is that this person is able to translate what she *doesn't* want into what she *does*. With a little practice, this can become easy and second nature, but often at first, it's awkward because of the thinking and communication patterns that we've established and practiced for a long time. For instance, I like to use the example of communicating with a small child. We say, "Don't slam the door!" and because the brain doesn't see the word "don't" we often get repeated slamming of the door. What we really want is for the child to close the door quietly as he comes into the house, but that's *not* what we asked for! Let's examine a model for converting undesirable behavior to desirable behavior and then share a process for doing this translation and conversion.

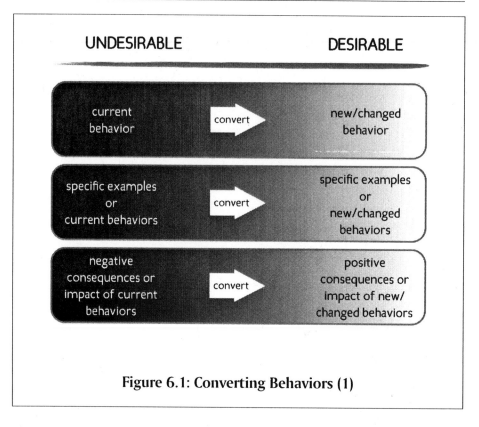

Figure 6.1: Converting Behaviors (1)

Step 1: First, identify the current behavior that seems to be causing the problem. What is it that they are doing that you don't like or want?

Step 2: What is the evidence of this? i.e. what are some examples of the specific behavior that is happening?

Step 3: What are the negative consequences of these behaviors? What's happening as a result that is undesirable?

Now, the conversion: when you examine what you've written in Step 1, do the following:

Step 4: What do you want them to do instead? What is the desirable behavior?

Step 5: What would it look like (the desirable behaviors) if it were what you wanted?

Step 6: What are the positive consequences that would occur if these new behaviors were present? Or, what are the likely positive consequences with the change?

Let's use the example of my conversation with the client regarding the VP of Sales:

Converting Behaviors (sample)

Undesirable	Desirable
Step 1: What's currently going on that's undesirable? *The VP of sales is not managing his team to make the goal numbers.*	Step 4: What do you want instead? *For the VP to successfully manage a high performing sales team.*
Step 2: What is the evidence? What are some examples? • *4 of his 6 sales execs were down during the last quarter's reporting.* • *He confronts the low performers, but nothing seems to change.* • *He seems surprised that people aren't making their numbers.*	Step 5: What would it look like if it were what you wanted? • *Sales numbers would increase by xyz percentage.* • *He'd know exactly how each member was performing throughout the quarter and plan for adjustments in strategy or tactics.* • *His low performers would either improve performance or be let go within a reasonable amount of time.*
Step 3: What are the negative consequences? • *Overall sales are down.* • *Reps aren't going to earn the higher commissions.* • *He's not going to get his bonus.* • *Team seems disengaged and unmotivated.* • *Our relationship is stressful.*	Step 6: What are the positive consequences? • *Sales would increase because he'd know more about the pipeline and be able to be more proactive.* • *Both the reps and he will earn higher pay overall with commissions and bonuses.* • *Increased enthusiasm and performance will motivate the team* • *Our relationship will improve and we'll be able to behave more strategically.*

None of this is particularly earth-shattering or complicated; however, what this helps us do is translate what we don't want into what we do so that we can actually ask for what we want instead of emphasizing what we don't want, don't like, and frankly, is already obvious.

What about you? Use the chart below to convert or translate something you don't want into something you do:

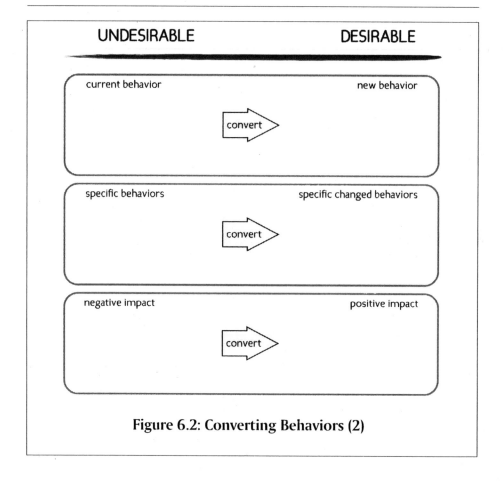

Figure 6.2: Converting Behaviors (2)

Using a Basic Influencing Request

Using the thinking and the specificity you've gained from clearly identifying and articulating what you want, it's helpful to have a methodology for actually asking for it—for having the conversation itself. You have the raw material to ask for what you want, but you may be able to increase your likelihood of being understood if you put some thought into *how* you'll ask for it.

WHAT = the information gained from your thinking, reflecting and translating what you don't like into what you want instead.

HOW = the methodology for having the conversation itself.

WHAT + HOW = Successful Influencing Request

For this reason, I offer a methodology (see fig. 6.3 and Chapter 8) that will help you organize your thoughts in such a way that you are able to accomplish the following:

1. Ask for what you really want, rather than what you don't want.
2. Ask for it in such a way that you are delivering high levels of the Core Dimensions, which increases trust and decreases defensiveness.

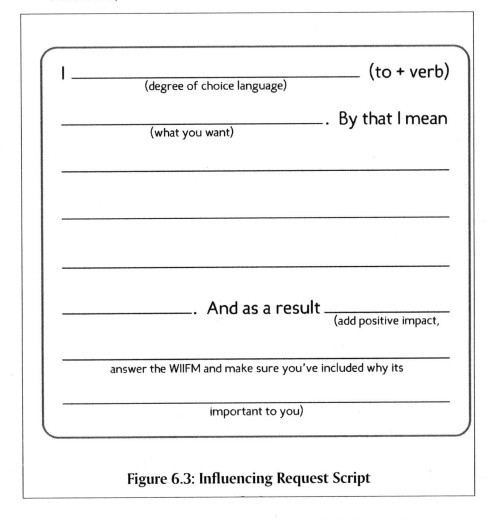

I _____ (to + verb)
(degree of choice language)

_____. By that I mean
(what you want)

_____

_____

_____

_____. And as a result _____
(add positive impact,

_____
answer the WIIFM and make sure you've included why its

_____
important to you)

Figure 6.3: Influencing Request Script

Now, at first, don't worry about whether or not this feels natural because it probably won't, but on the other hand, with practice, you integrate and internalize the skills and the thinking and it becomes a natural part of your communication style and habits.

Four Elements

There are four basic elements of a successful influencing request, and these answer the four subconscious questions someone has when we are trying to influence them or ask them to do something:

1. Who wants this?
2. Why do they want this?
3. What do you mean, exactly?
4. What's in it for me? Or why would I want to do this?

Notice the corresponding element for the Basic Influencing Request, below.

Question/Element Chart

Subconscious Question	Influencing Request Element
Who wants this?	Own it with an "I message"
Why do you want this?	Convey the importance with both language choice and specificity
What do you mean, exactly?	Be specific. Use examples, models, illustrations, etc.
What's in it for me? Why would I want to do this?	Share the impact: to the person, the organization or team, the group, the relationship, etc.

Element #1: Own it with an "I message"

Who wants this? You might assume, since most of the time a conversation is between two people, that the answer to this question would be obvious: the person sitting across from me is the person who wants this! However and especially in the workplace, this is not always how we approach asking for things, or influencing. Sometimes we are the messengers for asking. Sometimes we feel removed from the influencing request and are asking on the behalf of others. Unless you are the leader at the very top of the organization, or you own your business, chances are someone else, or a group of someones, like a board, shareholders, customers, people from another business unit or agency, etc. may be the initiators of the change request. It might not actually *be* you, so why not just say, "the boss wants this . . . " or "the board suggests that you . . ." or "headquarters is asking for . . ."?

Does it really matter if you phrase a request using the word "I"? Using "I" is the clearest, most direct way to communicate your frame of reference. It is also the quickest way to demonstrate Genuineness, so when we are engaged in a communication situation and we say, "I would like you to . . ." or "I need you to . . ." we are demonstrating our responsibility and ownership of the request, which feels more sincere to the person sitting across from us than pushing off the request on someone else who isn't there.

What if the request is really from a "we"? Even if that's true, the relationship, the conversation, is right now, at this moment, between you and the person with whom you are interacting. The context you build for the influencing request can contain the information that helps them understand, but the request, right now, is from you.

Isn't it much more difficult to say "no" to a real person sitting across from you, asking you one-on-one with respect? Wouldn't you rather someone "talk straight" to you and ask for what they want? Egotism is not based upon giving too many "I" messages; it is more about not listening to the other person and demonstrating a lack of empathy and respect. The beginning of your influencing request should begin with "I."

Element #2: Convey the Importance

Again, this might seem obvious. As with the example, above, it seems like the VP of sales would have to be pretty dense not to understand why the CEO would want him to improve his leadership of the sales team to increase its numbers, right? However, there are some subtleties here that can make all the difference. For example, if you examine the conversion chart, you'll see that if not explicitly stated, certainly the reasons for the request for change are implied. Here are some of the reasons that might be pertinent:

- The CEO wants to support the VP's growth and development as a leader and knows his ability to get results will impact how others perceive his own leadership.
- The CEO is stressed out by feeling that he has to worry about his VP's performance and is distracted from other strategic issues in leading the organization because he has to manage this issue.
- The CEO is wondering whether or not the VP is the right person in the role and needs to see improvement in overall performance.

Now, the CEO may not choose to include all or any of these reasons, but he can choose based on the situation at hand and the relationship he has with the VP. Regardless, the unanswered question about "why?" is important to address because it removes obstacles to understanding and to eventually resolving the issue or moving forward.

Degree of Choice Implied

Another important element here to consider is the actual language you choose which will also demonstrate the level of importance or urgency with regards to what you want. For example, if you use "I would like you to . . ." versus "I expect you to . . ." you set a very different tone and expectation for the person you are trying to influence. Neither one is right or wrong, but it is important that you select the one that is right for the situation, the relationship, and the power dynamic. Notice, in the following table, the lowest in assertion or control is at the bottom of the list, whereas the higher control language is at the top. You pick the one that is the most likely to convey your sense of importance.

Degree of Choice Language

Degree of Choice/Sense of Assertion Language
"I demand . . ."
"I expect . . ."
"I need . . ."
"I want . . ."
"I prefer . . . "
"I would like you to . . ."
"I would like you to consider . . ."
"I wonder if you could . . ."

Rarely will someone use "I demand," but it demonstrates the highest level of assertion and illustrates the softening of language as you move down the chart. This is not to say that if you select from the bottom of the list that you are making a weak or unimportant request. However, you will often choose what feels appropriate based on your own personal style, the power dynamic, the relationship status, the other person's likely response, etc. What feels right to you? What seems right for the situation?

Element #3: Be Specific

Hard to imagine that I could say anything more about Specificity that I've not already said, but it's one of the most important and significant elements of influencing and accelerates the speed with which you can create your Profit Culture. Let's just say it again: you're not specific enough. If you were, most of the time you'd get exactly what you want. People who know how to leverage Specificity not only get what they want at work, they arguably have a better quality of life. Sound strange? Think about the last time you traveled. Think of all the details and accommodations and how close they turned out with what you'd expected. Ask for what you want, be specific, and set the other person for success! It's that simple.

In a Basic Influencing Request, Specificity answers the question, "what would that look like?" If you take a look at the table below, you can see how often when we ask someone for something, we are too vague or general, yet we do it all the time and often don't get the results we want. You can probably add more details, but look at the examples below:

Specificity Table

What you want	"What would that look like?"
Be cooperative	• Ask for others' input • Collaborate on idea generating and decision-making • Be willing to hear someone out before discarding their idea • Find ways to say "yes" or create win-win
Be supportive	• Commit to our regular one-one meetings • Be willing to give me a "heads-up" if you see something that might affect the project • Take time to answer questions and/or explain or clarify
Be a good team player	• Demonstrate an ability to be flexible in your scheduling and shifts • Think "two steps ahead" and communicate with team if something might get our project off-track • Actively contribute to others' success by sharing information or best practices
Be more accurate or detail-oriented	• Carefully check work prior to submitting • Ask for help or assistance in plenty of time to make adjustments • Fewer than 5% errors
Be more timely	• Before Friday at 5 p.m. to submit change requests • On time for meetings; ready to go 5 minutes early • Consider others' timeframes when planning

What you want	"What would that look like?"
Be respectful	• Allow someone to finish speaking before sharing your ideas in conversation • Consider, by asking, someone else's time commitments before committing to an extra meeting • Be willing to negotiate or compromise for the good of the team or project
Be more courteous	• Use 'please' and 'thank-you' as appropriate • Clean up after yourself in the break room • Excuse yourself to take a call rather than talking over the meeting or group session
Clean your room (for your teenager!)	• All laundry clean, folded and put away • Floor vacuumed • Bed made • By Sunday night at 9 p.m.

Of course, there are a myriad of options for each, and each will depend upon the situation, person and exactly what you want them to do. Remember, high Specificity is not deemed condescending or belittling when it is delivered respectfully and with tact.

Element #4: Share the Impact

The final element of a Basic Influencing Request is to share the positive impact of the person's willingness to say "yes," or be influenced by you. Or, in other words, "here's the good stuff that will happen if you give me what I want!"

Positive versus Negative Impact

A lot of times people want to know why we focus on the positive when indeed sometimes there are negative consequences if the person says "no" to your request. Initially, in the Basic Influencing Request, you want to emphasize the positive because of a few things:

1. people are generally not motivated by negatives or threats
2. negatives or threats cause people to be defensive
3. focusing on the positives often increases trust and feels more respectful

Lest you imagine this is the Pollyanna method for influencing, let me assure you it's not—sometimes you need to share specific facts or information that is negative, but I find success in using these elements later in the conversation, only when necessary. This is why, from the beginning, it's good to convert the Undesirables to Desirables, including those consequences in Step 3 and 6 (Figure 6.1). That's what will help you prepare for this part of the Influencing Request.

Examine the following statements:

1. "I expect you to do a good job on this project. That way, I won't have to tell the boss you've been negligent."
2. "I need you to improve the quality of your reports so that we don't lose our raises this year."
3. "I would like you to stop being so difficult at our team meetings because no one wants to work with you on any of the upcoming projects."

But what if all these statements are *true?* Try to remember the difference between *respectful* honesty and *disrespectful* honesty. Generally, when others or we take pride in being "brutally honest," it means they don't care about how the other person will perceive their language or tone. Of course, this is fine, but just know the risk. If you make someone defensive right out of the gate, they're often not listening, defensive and not saying "yes" to your request.

Revised Statements

1. "I expect you to do a good job on this project, including getting all your work submitted on time, ensuring the professional quality and accuracy of the work, and meeting with me to debrief before we present the final report. That way, we'll both be assured of our success, the boss will be pleased with our project, and our next collaboration will have a blueprint for how we'll work together—so it'll take less time for you to prepare."
2. "I need you to improve the quality of your reports . . . I know if we are able to make this happen, we'll be on track for our raises and be set up for next quarter way ahead of time."
3. "I would like you to improve your participation and communication in team meetings . . . this will allow us to equally divide the workload for upcoming projects, you'll be assured to have strong people on your section, and it will minimize stress for all of us."

In the first one, I demonstrate some Specificity in the request itself. The others emphasize the positive consequences and the WIIFM for the listener.

In general there are two basic categories for positive consequences that will create an impact, and often they can overlap:

1. What is the positive impact to the team, organization, business unit, company, project, relationship, etc.?

2. What is the positive impact for this person him or herself? Generally, we call this the WIIFM factor—What's In It For Me?

Appeal to Enlightened Self-Interest

Even the most generous, altruistic person will evaluate whether or not they want to do something based upon the WIIFM factor. People, because they are unique, are motivated by very different things, but you can often identify some principles around the WIIFM factor. For example, most people value the following:

- They like to be seen as professionals.
- They like to be viewed as intelligent, savvy, and in-touch with what's going on.
- They like to be seen as confident and competent.
- They would prefer less stress in their lives.
- They often value being a good team member or contributor.
- They want to save face or minimize embarrassment or disappointment.

Of course, some of the WIIFM factor may be attributed to a specific situation or person. You may want to ask yourself, what does this person care about? Or what's the buy-in factor, i.e. what will help them have buy-in to an overall vision or view?

Instituting Change in an Individual

How do you get someone to change? Is it possible? It is important to note that instituting change can often take one of three forms:

1. **Coercion:** *you make someone do something.* Here's Position Power again; this often creates resistance and defensiveness and gains the short-term compliance rather than long-term commitment or change. It will typically damage trust.

2. **Peer Pressure**: *everyone else is doing it, so get on board!* This creates short-term change because peer pressure is fickle and moves with the wind—people are always changing their minds.

3. **Enlightened Self-Interest**: *you help someone align their personal pay-off with your goal for change.* This has a better chance of creating both long-term commitment and change and can impact trust in a positive way because the person believes that to make the change will create a better situation.

Remember, we can't make someone do something, but improving the way you influence, improving the way you "ask for what you want" will allow you to create a significant impact on your team, on those individual relationships, and ultimately on your organization as a whole.

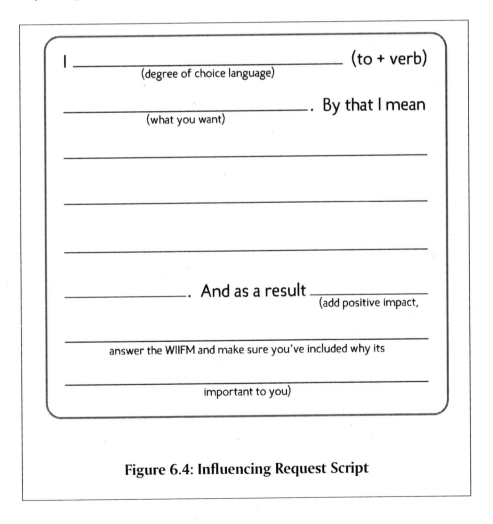

I _____ (to + verb)
(degree of choice language)

_____ . By that I mean
(what you want)

_____

_____

_____

_____ . And as a result _____
(add positive impact,

_____
answer the WIIFM and make sure you've included why its

_____
important to you)

Figure 6.4: Influencing Request Script

What does Chapter 6 have to do with building a Profit Culture?

One of the most important changes you can make to your leadership and communication is to utilize language that is efficient and effective—asking for what you want in a way that's easy to understand and say "yes" to will differentiate you as a leader and communicator.

Chapter 7

Stating the Obvious: Dealing with Issues and Confronting What Needs to Be Done

Why it's critical, crucial and otherwise essential for you to confront

Confrontation has gotten a bad rap. Here, now, at the beginning of this chapter, I want to declare confrontation is a *good* thing and is one of the most important skills you need as a leader. Because, when you don't confront, when you avoid it like the plague or at all costs (and all the other clichés people use to talk about confronting), you suffer, the other person suffers, your organization suffers. You damage your own credibility by being a poor or non-confronter.

But wait. We *hate* confrontational people . . . if not hate, then we at least try to avoid them because frankly, they're unpleasant when they are angry, up-in-your-face, neck veins bulging and temperature rising. Even if they're not losing their temper, the steely-eyed confrontations of former authority figures which created fear and our loathing the next conversation with them imprinted us forever. Or, we begrudgingly admit that sometimes, confrontation is necessary. It's uncomfortable and ugly, but that's why we get paid the big bucks, so we've gotta do it.

Nope, and nope. Confrontation, as we define it and use it in the Influencing Options® model, is respectful, direct, specific and very effective. Sometimes, people don't even feel confronted, and it's not because we're being sneaky or manipulative. Most of the time, when people have finished with an effective confronting conversation, what everyone feels is *relief*—relief to finally have an issue resolved, or a miscommunication averted, or an obstacle removed. Confrontation is good!

Bob Weyant, author of *Confronting without Conflict or Guilt: How to Prepare and Deliver a Confrontation in a Way that Minimizes Risk, Conflict and Guilt*, (2nd edition), notes that confronting well is a quality-of-life skill. I agree with his assertion (and I've experienced time and time again the evidence with my clients) that when we *need* to confront and we do *not* confront, there are some possible negative consequences:

- We may continue to be distressed and fester, which may lead to either a "blow up" where we confront in an emotional, reactive way, or we hold it in which can make us ill.
- We may get only temporary relief by complaining (aka venting) to friends and colleagues, and they're not the ones who need to be confronted anyway.
- The person will likely continue the negative, undesirable behavior because they don't know anything's wrong, and often, they just get better at whatever they're doing that we don't like!

Confronting is a subset of influencing when we examine the Influencing Sequence (Chapter 9) and the Three Effective Choices (Chapter 1—it's one of the ways we may need to deal with an issue or a problem.

Earlier in Chapters 1 and 4, I described The Differentiation Factor—the two things that seemed to recur over and over in my coaching of executive clients. The two factors that separated the leaders who soar from the leaders who struggle:

Differentiator 1: Clearly articulate your vision and create alignment among your followers.

Differentiator 2: Confront issues quickly, directly and respectfully.

Confronting issues quickly, directly and respectfully

Leaders need to respond thoughtfully and immediately to issues that arise that may impact business results—interpersonal conflict, performance issues, stalled team processes, poor ethics, breaches in customer service. Candor and honesty are the important currency of good leadership—*the art is in the delivery.*

Ineffective confrontation is often volatile and blaming. It is not future-focused and, instead, often damages the relationship between the leader and the other person. It creates wreckage and metaphorical body parts strewn alongside the road. It can paralyze a team, mask talent and skill, and sabotage the best efforts for success. Effective confrontation is direct, specific, and respectful. It is the perfect execution of the balancing act mentioned before—holding people accountable while demonstrating respect. Effective confrontation can actually increase trust in a relationship and decrease defensiveness—it goes hand-in-hand with effective influencing skills and helps to create an atmosphere of commitment, accountability, and teamwork.

Confrontation: A New Definition

If effective confrontation is *a respectful request for a new behavior or behavior change*, we can confront situations and issues that arise in our organizations with candor and transparency. Often, we hesitate to confront someone because we fear to do so will make the relationship worse or our perceived risk is high. We may think that the person's reaction will be emotional or angry and we may go to great lengths to avoid the situation, the person, and the conversation. We may even leave a job or a relationship unnecessarily because we are so fearful of the potential conflict and we cannot bear the stress and pain of the situation. Sound dramatic or drastic? We all know situations like this! Often, the real reason we don't confront is that we don't feel confident that we can pull it off well—that it will work and the potential bad consequences will be averted.

Confrontation does not have to involve conflict, and even though ultimately, we are powerless over people, we can prepare to have a conversation that confronts negative or undesirable behavior in a way that feels respectful to the person and to ourselves. If we confront, we must be willing to pay the price of the confrontation, which could be potential conflict or negative consequences; if we choose not to confront, we must be willing to pay the price of accepting the situation as it is.

An ideal situation for a confrontation conversation is to meet with the person privately, one-on-one, to ask for what you want or need. Cubicles aren't especially conducive to this type of confrontation. Confronting a whole group of people is risky, too, because most of the time, someone in that group is not applicable and you run the risk of alienating them. Confronting on e-mail *never* works. I rarely say *never*, but I've just never seen or heard of a time that confronting over e-mail has been successful, especially if *we define success as resolving an issue, respectfully so that it increases trust and decreases defensiveness*. Most of the time, when someone sends a "flaming" e-mail, where they CC God and everybody, the results range from devastating to distracting, at the least. It just doesn't work.

Examine the table to compare the elements of an effective confrontation versus an ineffective confrontation:

Confrontations

Effective	Ineffective
In person, in private	In a group or over e-mail
Positive nonverbals	Negative or mixed message nonverbals
No excess emotional baggage	Excess emotional baggage
"I" messages	Blaming with "you" statements
Focused on desirable behaviors	Focused on undesirable behaviors
Focused on positive consequences and results	Focused on negative consequences or threats

Prepare for a Successful Confrontation

You can set the stage for a productive confrontation conversation by considering the elements listed in the above table:

In person, in private

If at all possible, meet with the person one-on-one in a private setting. If your office has cubicles or is not conducive for a private conversation, go somewhere else! Imagine how you would like someone else to have an important conversation with you—probably not out in the open or in front of others.

> *Less effective: Generally, people do not like to be confronted in a group. This may cause embarrassment, resistance or even anger, and that will not contribute to increasing trust and decreasing defensiveness. Confrontation over e-mail, as mentioned, is not only ineffective, it's often disrespectful and a breeding ground for miscommunication and misinterpretation. You give up all the nonverbals of a face-to-face conversation and have to rely solely on your words in text. Even over the phone is better because at least you can hear one another's voices and have the back-and-forth of listening and talking.*

Positive Nonverbals

Your facial expression, tone of voice and mannerisms all communicate something to the other person. Even though there are some cultural differences among people with regards to nonverbal communication, we generally believe that making eye contact means we are focused, engaged, and respectful. Attending behaviors, such as a slight incline forward of the body and an open facial expression also help to demonstrate respect.

> *Less effective: Either loud or very soft speaking can send a mixed message. Closed body posture, arms crossed, etc. can communicate a lack of openness. Distracting behaviors, such as leg jiggling or pen clicking can be irritating and reduce focus. Being too close or too far away (2-3 feet is generally appropriate for a focused, important conversation) can impede communication also. Pay attention, also to where you are: if you have a desk between you and the person you are confronting, you have already set up your "defense" in terms of nonverbal communication. Come out from behind the desk.*

No excess emotional baggage

To maintain control in a confrontation conversation, you want to keep calm and focused on the specific issue at hand. If this is a challenging relationship, don't bring up everything this person has ever done that has been disappointing or upsetting to you. Don't engage your dinosaur brain. Preparing for the conversation will help reduce the potential for becoming overly emotional or getting your buttons pushed.

> *Less effective: Even if you are a normally expressive person, allowing yourself to become overly emotional will either put the person on the defensive or they may perceive that you are angry or overreacting to a situation and interpret your request as unimportant.*

Using "I" messages

Own your thoughts, ideas and feelings. Use "I" to help the person understand what you want and what you need rather than using generalizations.[29]

> *Less effective: Using "you" and blaming is generally a sure way to create a defensive, less productive conversation. "You did this . . ." and "you did that . . ." creates an immediate adversarial atmosphere.*

Focused on desirable behaviors

An effective confrontation focuses on **what you want** rather than what you don't want and gives examples of the desired behavior so that they know exactly what you are asking for.

> *Less effective: Focusing on the undesirable behaviors creates two potential problems. One is that it feels like blaming to the other person, so the potential for defensiveness and resistance is high. The other is that when you focus on the undesirable behavior you create a more clear picture of what you do not want and that is what becomes embedded in the mind. You can actually make it worse!*

Focused on positive consequences and results

This, again, is appealing to the person's self interest or common vision by introducing the WIIFM (What's in it for me?) factor. People generally want to believe that if they make a change as a result of your confrontation, something will improve about the situation and things will be better.

> *Less effective: People, in general, are not motivated by or deterred by negative consequences or threats because it feels heavy-handed, threatening, or an abuse of Position Power. It's another sure-fire way to increase defensiveness in the person you are confronting.*

---

29   For a more detailed discussion, see Chapter X, Ask for What You Want .

A Confrontation Continuum: Three Options for Confronting

Following is a description and a script for three types of confrontations: Discrepancy Confrontation, Behavior Request, Accountability Confrontation. In general, you want to keep the following in mind as you decide what your confrontation strategy will be:

1. Delivering high levels of the Core Dimensions during your confrontation is essential. This means you need to be purposefully delivering high levels of Respect, Empathy, Specificity and Genuineness during the interaction.

2. You can start or end anywhere on the continuum; you do not need to use all three confrontations, and often you will resolve the issue before moving to the next level.

3. Pay close attention to your language use. The greatest risk in confronting is making someone defensive, which means their listening can shut down. Emphasize the positive aspects first, then, if you need to, you can share examples of the undesirable behaviors that have happened in the past.

4. Sometimes creating context or framing helps to set the tone for the conversation. Two particularly powerful phrases that I use and suggest to my coaching clients are: "I've been thinking a lot about this," which suggests the genuine importance of the conversation, and "I need your help," which can decrease defensiveness and encourage closer listening.

Comparing the Confrontation Options: Definitions

Here are some suggestions of when to use and when not to use the different options:

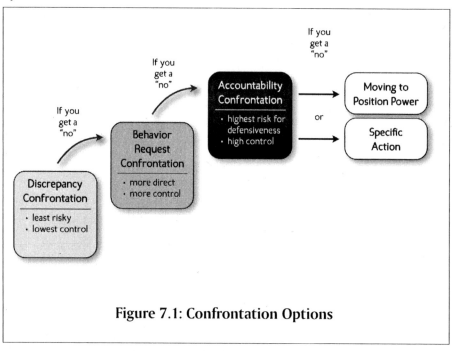

Figure 7.1: Confrontation Options

Confrontations: When to Use (or not)

Option	When to use it	When not to use it
Discrepancy	You perceive the conversation as high-risk, either to create defensiveness or because of the power dynamic; you need more information; there is a mis-match between what is currently happening and either what has happened before or what the person said would happen	When you've had this conversation before—you may be perceived as insincere or inattentive if you're too far along in the process of what has happened.

Option	When to use it	When not to use it
Behavior Request	You want to make a direct request for the change you want or need, providing specifics.	When to do so would create initial defensiveness in the person because you do not have any context or enough information
Accountability	You are moving toward using Position Power, i.e. last resort. Or, you have a sense of urgency with the issue because your next step is purposeful action	When to do so would create only short-term compliance; when it's too risky to diminish trust.

Discrepancy Confrontation

The Discrepancy Confrontation is one of the most useful tools in the Influencing Options® model because it is a low risk, low control confrontation. It is often a way to enter into a confrontation conversation in order to gain more information or additional insight. It may be a larger time investment, initially, because you are initiating a conversation to begin.

The confrontation has four parts:

1. **Your feeling about the discrepancy.** I typically advise a few neutral feeling words up front: *concerned, confused or frustrated.* Of course, you can name any feeling you want that's sincere about how you really are feeling. These three allow you to enter in without the emotional attachment that words such as *angry, disappointed or disturbed* might elicit. You choose.

2. **The past behavior or agreement.** The Discrepancy Confrontation works because it points out an obvious mis-match. Either, the past behavior, which was desirable (like good communication or strong performance) is no longer the case, or an agreement you made about a decision, path or follow-through is not being upheld. If you are citing a positive past behavior, you must make sure and describe it using Specificity, or you will be perceived as insincere, or non-Genuine.

3. **The current behavior or distinction.** What is going on now? Be specific and factual from your point of view or your experience. What's going on now doesn't match up with what you expected or had been led to believe about what would happen.

4. **An *implied* open-ended question.** "Implied" is important here. You don't actually put the question, i.e. "what's going on?" or " can you tell me what's up?" at the end of your confrontation because in this situation we are really minimizing the potential for defensiveness. The question is implied, as you will see in the examples, below. What you do include is a very purposeful pause. Say nothing and wait for their response.

Here are some examples:

1. *"Jody, I'm concerned because on the one hand, you've told me about your professional goals to promote to a higher position with greater authority and pay, yet on the other hand, you've been consistently late to our team meetings."*

2. *"Tom, I'm frustrated because I thought the last time we spoke you had agreed to get back to me each Friday with a progress report and I've not heard from you in over three weeks."*

3. *"Joe, I'm confused because on the one hand, you are the top performer on our team. Your attention to detail, your timeliness and the quality of your work are models for all of the new engineers. Yet, on the other hand, often your interactions with co-workers are stressful and tense."*

4. *"Mary, I'm confused because on the one hand, you have entrusted me with the management of this project and that shows a sincere demonstration in supporting my development as a leader. Yet on the other hand, I feel like you are concerned about my follow-through when I receive multiple calls and e-mails each day checking on the progress of the project and what I'm doing."*

You can see that each of the statements is relatively low risk, respectful and could create a potential opening for a conversation to begin. ***Sometimes this is all you need!*** The person says, "you know, you're right," or "actually, I've been meaning to talk to you about this," or "wow! I had no idea." The important thing to remember when delivering a Discrepancy Confrontation is to be fully present so you can listen and deliver empathy. This will set the tone for the conversation and aid you in strengthening or preserving the relationship.

Behavior Request Confrontation

A Behavior Request is a direct and respectful request for the desired behavior change and the very same structure as the basic Influencing Request (Chapter 6). The only thing that might be different in delivering a basic Influencing Request and a Behavior Request is the context—the former can be about something entirely new and the latter is really about change.

If you begin the conversation with the Discrepancy Confrontation and the person's response to you is essentially a "no" or denial, you have the choice of increasing your influencing power (or upping the control) by being more direct. Even if you are going to begin your conversation with the Discrepancy Confrontation, you may also want to prepare your Behavior Request so that you are ready to ask for what you want directly and not have to rely on an additional conversation.

Remember, the successful Behavior Request has the same four parts as the Basic Influencing Request:

1. Own it with an "I" statement
2. Convey the importance
3. Be specific
4. Share the impact

For your conversation, you will also want to have at least two examples of the undesirable behaviors tucked in your back pocket just in case the person acts confused, i.e. *what do you mean by that?* Or, *can you give me an example?* Don't play these cards first, as you will likely create initial defensiveness. You may not need to use them at all, but you should be prepared.

Here are some Behavior Requests using the Discrepancy Confrontation examples, above:

1. **Discrepancy**: *"Jody, I'm concerned because on the one hand, you've told me about your professional goals to promote to a higher position with greater authority and pay, yet on the other hand, you've been consistently late to our team meetings."*

   Behavior Request: *"Jody, I would like you to be on time for our team meetings. By that I mean, at the conference table ready to go by 8 a.m. As a result, you'll get to participate fully, I'll be assured of your commitment to our team, your team members will feel respected, and you'll be setting the example for high professional standards."*

2. **Discrepancy**: *"Tom, I'm frustrated because I thought the last time we spoke you had agreed to get back to me each Friday with a progress report and I've not heard from you in over three weeks."*

   Behavior Request: *"Tom, I expect you to submit to me a progress report for our project by Monday noon each week until completion. That way, I'll be able to track our results, identify where you might need more resources or time, and we'll all be set to meet our deadlines as a team."*

3. **Discrepancy**: *"Joe, I'm confused because on the one hand, you are the top performer on our team. Your attention to detail, your timeliness and the quality of your work are models for all of the new engineers. Yet, on the other hand, often your interactions with co-workers are stressful and tense."*

   Behavior Request: *"Joe, I would like you to improve your communication with your team members. By that I mean, speaking calmly and respectfully when interacting, allowing someone to fully share an idea before sharing your own, and increasing the time you spend to explain procedures to our new team members. As a result, you'll be seen as the expert professional, your team members will treat you with more respect, your stress will decrease because they'll be more likely to support your efforts, and I'll be able to concentrate on getting the additional resources we need for the new projects."*

4. **Discrepancy**: *"Mary, I'm confused because on the one hand, you have entrusted me with the management of this project and that shows a sincere demonstration in supporting my development as a leader. Yet on the other hand, I feel like you are concerned about my follow-through when I receive multiple calls and e-mails each day checking on the progress of the project and what I'm doing."*

   Behavior Request: *"Mary, I would like you to give me more autonomy on this project. By that I mean, allowing me to manage my time and tasks, supporting me by meeting with me once a week to discuss progress and giving me some discrepancy when making decisions mid-project. As a result, I will be able to develop in my role as a project manager, you will spend less time having to follow upon me, and we'll create a stronger collaboration for future projects."*

TMI (Too Much Information?)

Sometimes, when people are learning the Influencing Skills model they wonder if the Behavior Request, with its level of specificity and detail might be too much information. Remember that while you are learning the elements of an effective Confrontation or Influencing Request, it is helpful to use a script to make sure you don't leave anything out. In reality, you will begin to integrate these skills and tools into your own style and thinking and you won't create a barrage of details to overwhelm the person. If you consider the example #4, perhaps a conversation might go something like this[30]:

You: *You know, Joe, I've been thinking a lot about what happened yesterday at our team meeting and I wanted to talk to you about it.*

Joe: *What do you mean? That little tiff with Jerry?*

You: *Yes, that's one example. You know, **I'm concerned because on the one hand, you're the top guy on our team. Your skills and expertise are the model for the quality of work I want everyone to aspire to. On the last project, for example, you really set the standard for innovation and quick turnaround.**"[31]*

Joe: *Thanks. It was a good project, wasn't it?*

You: *Yes, it was, and I certainly want us to continue to perform at that level—all of us. But that's not what concerns me. I'm concerned that even though your technical expertise is top notch, **your interactions with your team members are often stressful, tense and even contentious. It doesn't match up with your strong commitment to the good work you do.**[32]*

Joe: *What do you mean? I get the work done, that should be all that counts. I can't help it if some people are too sensitive or slackers!*

You: *Yes, you do get the work done, and that's very important to me, to the team and to the company, but I also need us to be able to work effectively and efficiently as a team because that will impact how we're able to reach our goals. **I need you to improve your***

---

30   Note the emboldened sections are the actual parts of the request that you would prepare and
      practice with a script. Here, they are fully integrated into a regular conversation.
31   Here's the first part of the Discrepancy Confrontation.
32   Here's the second part of the Discrepancy Confrontation.

communication with your team members[33] *so that we can decrease the time we spend distracted by stressful interactions.*

Joe: *I'm not sure what you're talking about. I'm paid to be an engineer, not a babysitter!*

You: *I'm not asking you to baby-sit your co-workers; I'm asking you to* **demonstrate more respect when you are interacting with them, and by that I mean, speaking calmly and respectfully when you're conveying something; listening and allowing someone to finish a thought before rushing in to state yours—even with Jerry! As a result, you'll be seen as not only the expert, go-to guy, but also you will increase your team members' respect of you and they'll be more willing to support your efforts on projects, as well. Additionally, if I know that things are running smoothly in the lab, then I can concentrate on securing additional funding for our next project, which we all can benefit from.**[34]

And so on. In other words, this type of conversation does not have to come out all in one exhalation of breath to bowl the person over with details. Integrate the effective strategies into the way a normal conversation precedes. This is also why, in general, if you are planning to have a confrontation conversation, you need to set aside a bit of time. Five minutes on the fly may not be enough to get the results you want.

Accountability Confrontation

If you choose to use the highest level of control in a confrontation conversation, you may want to use an Accountability Confrontation. Your main goal here is to get a clear "yes" or "no" quickly. No matter what the response, you translate it into a "yes" or "no" until the person becomes accountable.

For example

You: *"I need to know if you are willing to make some changes in the quality of your written reports, yes or no?"*

---

33   Here's the beginning of the Behavior Request.
34   Here's the specificity, and the other elements of the full Behavior Request.

Sam: *"I've already worked on these reports for the last week!"*

You: *"So, what you're saying is that you are not willing to improve the quality of your written reports?"*

Sam: *"No, that's not what I'm saying. I'm saying I feel like I've already worked on these enough."*

You: *"So because you feel like you've already worked on these enough, you're telling me that you're not willing to improve the quality?"*

Sam: *"No, I guess I could make some minor changes."*

You: *"So, you are willing to make some improvements?"*

And so on. It's easy to see how an Accountability Confrontation essentially forces the person to give you a "yes" or a "no" but you also run the risk of their becoming defensive and simply compliant. You may, however, have already tried a Discrepancy Confrontation, a Behavior Request and you are moving more toward using Position Power because you feel like it's the last resort. Also, once you get your clear "yes" or "no" you'll need to decide what your next step or choice may be.

On the following page, you'll see a worksheet that will allow you to build your confrontations by starting at the bottom of the page with Discrepancy and moving to the top of the page with Accountability.

Three P's for Remaining Calm and Confident: Facing the Tough Conversations

Sometimes we dread having those conversations that we really need to have: confronting a client, addressing an issue with an employee, or even resolving a problem with someone in our personal lives. My goal in these situations is to remain **Calm and Confident**.

Here are Three P's for Challenging Conversations:

1. **Preparation:** spend some time preparing for your conversation. Ask yourself, "what do I really want?" Often, we ask for what we don't want by confronting someone focusing on the undesirable behaviors. Jot down some talking points, think about what the best outcome could possibly be and concentrate on that. Vent elsewhere! If the person is defensive immediately, they're less likely to listen or participate fully in the conversation with you.

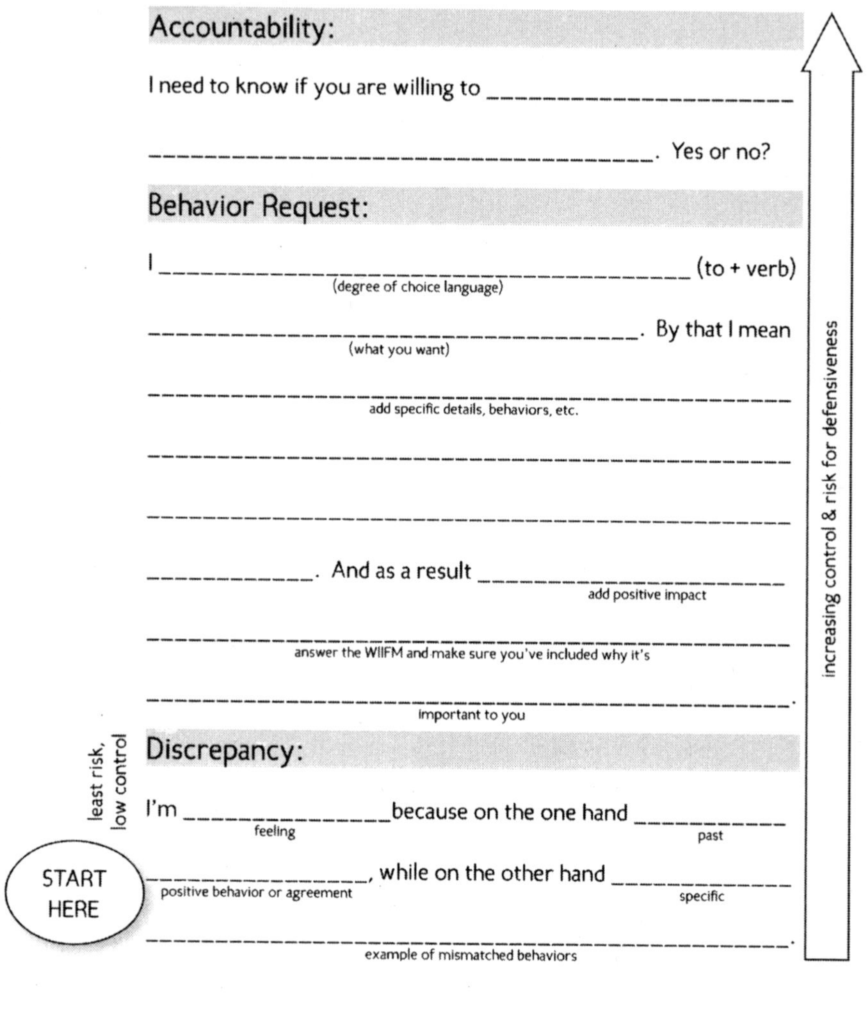

Accountability:

I need to know if you are willing to _____

_____. Yes or no?

Behavior Request:

I _____ (to + verb)
    (degree of choice language)

_____. By that I mean
    (what you want)

_____
    add specific details, behaviors, etc.

_____

_____

_____. And as a result _____
                                   add positive impact

_____
    answer the WIIFM and make sure you've included why it's

_____
    important to you

Discrepancy:

I'm _____because on the one hand _____
        feeling   past

_____, while on the other hand _____
    positive behavior or agreement   specific

_____
    example of mismatched behaviors

least risk, low control (rotated left label)

START HERE

increasing control & risk for defensiveness (rotated right label)

Figure 7.2: Scripts

2. **Practice:** plan what you're going to say, how you're going to listen, and how you think they might respond to you. Practice with a trusted friend or advisor and ask for feedback, especially around specificity and whether or not you're using any language that is blaming. The more comfortable you are with your own language in the moment, the less likely you'll be to have your own buttons pushed and the more likely you'll be to remain Calm and Confident.

3. **Plexi-glass**: envision a plexi-glass shield . . . for your emotional protection. Remember that you never have to be reactive, defensive, hurt or angry—you choose those emotions in a situation. If this person is likely (because they've done so in the past) to push your buttons or provoke you, your preparation and practice will allow you to be centered, in-the-moment and focused. You can select some phrases such as "I'm committed to having a positive, productive working relationship with you," or "I am committed to creating a win-win situation for both of us," or whatever the overall outcome or goal is within this relationship, to keep you grounded and calm.

What does Chapter 7 have to do with building a Profit Culture?

Since not dealing with issues, dealing with them poorly or letting things go on too long are all symptoms of Organizational Drag—the antithesis of Profit Cultures, confronting well—respectfully, directly and specifically—will differentiate you among leaders. That will impact your bottom line.

Chapter 8

Entering and Embracing the Conversation: Creating and Influencing Specific Relationships

Changing the World

For a short time, I worked for the Department of Corrections. Never mind I didn't really know anything about this industry when I began. Never mind that I never got comfortable visiting prison, no matter how many times I got buzzed through the gates in electric fences swathed in coils of razor wire. Never mind that I might literally be the only poet who volunteered for a hostage role-play and got shot twenty-five times with simunitions, when I don't even really like guns. It's probably safe to say that in general there weren't many poets amongst the employee ranks, but there I was.

In the beginning, I had a poet's fascination with this work: what are the reaches of the human spirit, the human condition, human choices and actions? I never got used to seeing men in waist chains hooked together in lines of orange jumpsuits. When I actually worked with offenders, which I didn't do very often, it was easy to see how some might say, "*but for the grace of God, there go I . . .*" and how other times I struggled cognitively with the *why* of some crimes committed. My last official assignment was to create a curriculum on preventing prison rape. It's easy to see now why I could never do this job for long.

I was an administrator, a manager and a leader, so I attended a lot of meetings. At one such meeting, I was preparing to interact with a new group of people who were rolling out a new program for supervising offenders after they had been released into the community corrections program, previously called probation and parole. This group talked constantly in acronyms and jargon, so it was difficult for me to track what we were even discussing, much less contribute much value.

We finally took a break and everyone filled their coffee cups and gathered around the bagels and fruit. In an attempt to catch up or at least gain some ground on understanding, I approached one of the men who seemed the most friendly and accessible—he was high energy, smiled, seemed enthusiastic about his work, and the conversation we were having in the group. Now, I don't even remember exactly what I asked him, but it was probably something like, "so . . . we're really trying to utilize this assessment tool to figure out whether or not someone is likely to reoffend?"

"No!" he said with great gusto, "we are changing the world!"

I have never forgotten that short exchange, not so much because of where I was, my job, or the project at hand, but because indeed, in some small or large ways, the conversations we are having at work are about changing the world, and I have embraced my own mission to change the world, one conversation at a time, when I work with leaders and their teams. David Whyte is absolutely right when he says, "the conversation is not *about* the work. The conversation *is* the work.[35]"

The Conversations

Oh, I know some of you were *so* hoping that wasn't actually the answer. I know that some were hoping that the whole darn thing, the absolute nugget of truth was that it was going to be about the bottom line, or the elaborate system, or the data we collect and analyze, or the innovative and exciting new products and services. It's not. It's about that moment, that space, created between you and someone else that fills up with the exchange of language, understanding and misunderstanding, brilliant ideas and devastating discoveries—the conversations with your customers, employees, team members, bosses, volunteers or vendors. What are you not yet talking about? What are the courageous conversations you are not having? Because if you're not having them, you cannot change the world, leave a legacy, or even make the next sale.

What does this have to do with building a Profit Culture?

1. Your conversations, and the artful (or not) navigation of them will determine whether or not you can influence others to follow you toward the Mission/Vision of your organization.

---

35   I've heard him say this in multiple places, interviews and recordings. See resources for an interview about "courageous conversations."

2. Your ability to influence, to get what you want or need while creating trust, determines your ability to create strong relationships, which will ultimately determine your success.

3. The leaders and companies willing to engage in these important, courageous conversations are the ones that cultivate environments where transparency, honesty and truth can emerge—the fertile ground for Profit Cultures.

4. If you cannot, or will not, engage in the conversations you need to have (even if they are with your own self), they will become insurmountable obstacles deterring you from all the good you can create as a leader and a person.

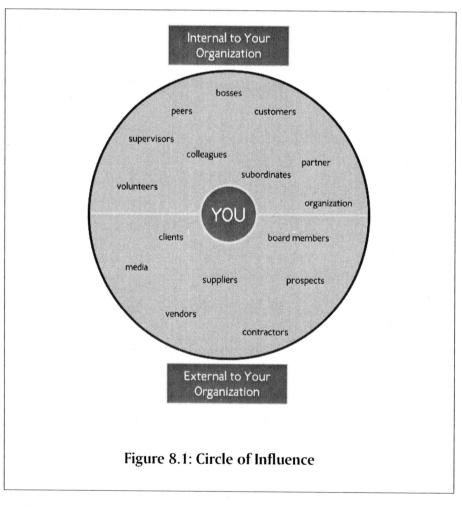

Figure 8.1: Circle of Influence

Brass Tacks

Let's get down to it, then. What are these conversations, and with whom do you need to have them? Most likely, the people within your immediate circle of influence are those with whom you are often interacting, collaborating or negotiating. Take a look at the circle in figure 8.1.

Notice there are people both internal and external to the organization that are in your circle of influence. Some of these may not apply to you, so use the blank one, included, and take some time to jot down the following:

1. Who are the people with whom you normally interact?
2. Who receives either the results of your work or your direction?
3. On whom do you rely to be successful in your work?
4. Whose actions/interactions can have a significant impact on you?

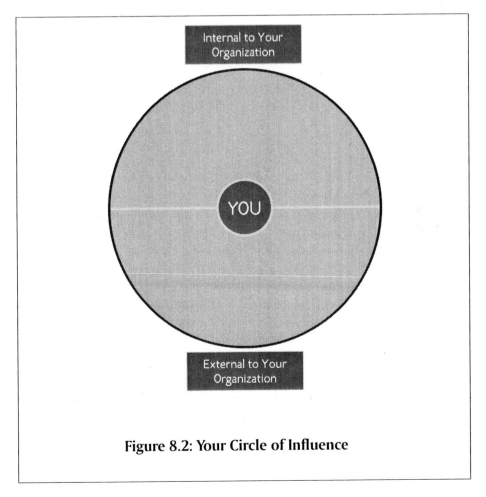

Figure 8.2: Your Circle of Influence

These, and probably more, are in your circle of influence, and therefore you are often in conversation with them. Conversation, by the way, can be any or all of the following:

1. in person
2. via e-mail
3. over the telephone, Skype or web conferencing
4. speaking from the podium
5. non-verbally interacting (as in a meeting where you might not even speak)
6. in writing

Influencing with Integrity

In our classes, workshops, seminars and webinars[36], we help people actually build and strengthen their conversation skills as influencers. Here in this book we introduce and discuss some of these particular tools and concepts, as well as introduce a philosophy for leading a Profit Culture. Some of the tools included here are:

- Creating a specific Influencing Request (i.e. Asking for What You Want)
- The Confrontation Continuum (Confronting effectively)
- Using Three Effective Choices
- Delivering the Core Dimensions

Influencing, in particular, is a specific type of conversation and one that you will enter again and again as a leader building a Profit Culture. You have a goal in mind—some sort of change you'd like to occur—and so the dynamic is heightened. It's not just a casual exchange of ideas or a brainstorming session. You want something to happen. If you're good at influencing with integrity, you get people to do what you want or need them to do while increasing trust and decreasing defensiveness. The reason this model for influencing works is that it's based on the simultaneous delivery of the Core Dimensions while you're asking for what you want.

Five Steps in the Influencing Sequence

This is a model of the basic Influencing Skills *process* that we teach in our Influencing Options® courses where we utilize a conceptual model[37] for teaching. Here, in this

---

36   Please visit www.libbywagner.com to find out more about specific professional development opportunities.
37   If you'd like to see a video that gives an overview of the conceptual model, log into www.libbywagner.com/videos/ismodel to check it out!

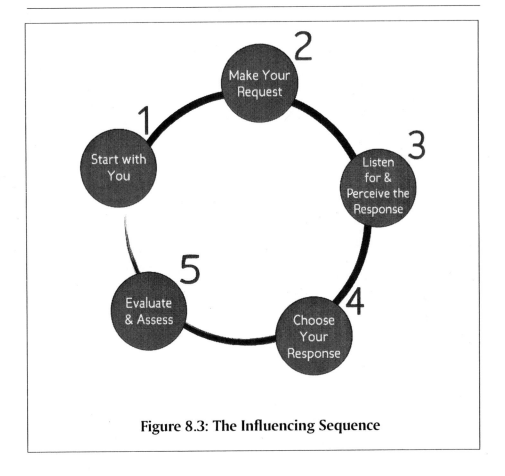

Figure 8.3: The Influencing Sequence

book, we are taking a look at how to use it in the context of leading, and especially how it can impact your ability to create a Profit Culture for your organization. The concepts are very simple; the execution is not so difficult once you understand and can internalize the elements. The toughest thing about using this model is to use it with discipline and commitment, and that is your biggest leverage for creating the culture you want—the one that supports high levels of productivity, trust, morale, customer delight, profits, low turnover, less stress and increased happiness at work. Remember also, that this really isn't a formula—conversing with others isn't always very neat and tidy—yet it offers specific guidelines and tools for creating the strongest foundation for an open, respectful and specific conversation: the kind that can influence Profit Cultures.

Preparing to Influence

The feedback I often hear, other than, "this works[38]," is "I can't believe how easy that was because I was prepared." Again, it seems so obvious, but often we go into the challenging conversation sort of hoping for the best, steeling up for the worst. Generally, it goes a lot better if we prepare and even practice.

Step 1: Start with You

The process of influencing a Profit Culture is greatly improved when you practice the Core Dimension of *Specificity* on yourself! You need to gain clarity about what you want, specifically. Here are four Helpful Questions to get you thinking about influencing:

1. What, exactly, do you want them to do? Convert undesirable to desirable[39], if necessary.

2. How important is this to you? Why do you want them to do this?

3. What are the positive consequences—the good stuff—that are likely to occur if they say 'yes' to your request? How will it impact the team, organization, project, relationship, etc.?

4. What's in it for them? How will they benefit or gain?

Answering all of these questions will help you prepare your raw material, especially in terms of Specificity and positive language.

The Other Person

It also helps, in preparation, to think about the person you are trying to influence. I like to use Aristotle's rhetorical triangle—even if I do so in my head— (see figure 8.4) to take a look at what I might need to consider when I am thinking about the other person.

Simply put, Aristotle suggested that in any communication situation, there are three elements:

1. you
2. the other person
3. the issue/topic (or what you want to happen)

---

38   Actually, one of my very favorite responses to my after-the-first-session query, "Well, how did your practice go?" was from Erin in Colorado who said, "Holy Crap! This works!"
39   See Figures 6.1 and 6.2.

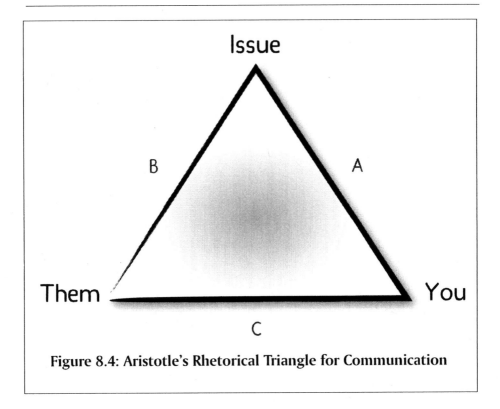

Figure 8.4: Aristotle's Rhetorical Triangle for Communication

The relationships between the various angles in the triangle allow us to examine the dynamics we need to think about. For example, in A, you are really answering questions 1 and 2, in the Helpful Questions, above. You are examining the relationship between you and the outcome of what you want—your ideas, history, feelings, sense of urgency, why you want it, etc. You need to know this information so that you can do two things: prepare to influence and prepare to answer questions during the conversation itself.

For B, you examine the relationship between the outcome of what you want and try to think about how the other person might view it, or what their attachment or non-attachment is to it—their position, opinions, feelings, history, what they care about, etc. The more you know about this, the better prepared you can be not only to see things from their vantage point, which will help you be a better listener, but also so that you can anticipate what their concerns or objections might be.

For C, you take a look at the relationship between you and the other person, as it currently exists: do you have commitment to shared vision? What is your trust level? Do you know them at all, or do you have a long-time history with them? What is important about creating some common ground between the two of you, and is there room for a "win-win" scenario?

Step 2: Make Your Request

Use the extensive information in Chapter 6, "By that I mean: Asking for What You Want," because it will help you really get the nitty gritty of converting undesirable behavior and clarifying your real objectives. Remember, these are the Four Elements of a successful Influencing Request:

1. Own it with an "I" message
2. Convey the importance
3. Be specific
4. Share the impact

Here is a practice script for you that will accomplish the following:

1. You will make sure to include all of the four elements.
2. You will increase your chances for high Specificity.
3. You will prepare this in alignment with high Core Dimensions.
4. You will have something to practice and refine before the real conversation.

At first, this may seem awkward and unnatural because it's not the way you usually converse. One of the reasons why I enjoy the light-hearted mocking I sometimes get from class participants, i.e. "well, *by that I mean . . . !*" or "*in the spirit of specificity . . .*" is that this means they are internalizing the concepts and thinking about them and using them! The script helps with internalizing until you can remember the elements and the language and use it in your own style of speaking. It works.

Step 3: Listen and Perceive the Response

Once you have made your request, you've begun the conversation in this particular way, you need to be quiet next. This is more challenging for some than others. Certainly I have been the former for most of my life. I subscribed to the belief that if there were pregnant pauses or prolonged silences, it must mean the other person needed to hear more from me—needed additional information, so I kept talking! How can I hear someone's response, how can it be a conversation, if I'm the only one talking? To converse is to exchange, therefore, there must be two. Listening is essential.

I _____ (to + verb)
(degree of choice language)

_____ . By that I mean
(what you want)

_____

_____

_____

_____ . And as a result _____
(add positive impact,

_____

answer the WIIFM and make sure you've included why its

_____

important to you)

Figure 8.5: Influencing Request Slip

Perceiving is essential, too, because you need to know whether the person is responding with a "yes" or a "no" to your request because once you know this, you can choose from a variety of responses and options you have to move the influencing process forward. Here are some key elements in perceiving someone's response:

1. **Determine how much "yes" or "no" you are getting**. Sometimes people will say, "let me get back to you," or "yeah, great idea, but my plate is really full right now," or "oh, glad you brought that up . . . I wanted to talk to you about something else . . . " These are generally smoke screens or ways to say "no" without saying "no." Often, we think we

got a "yes," walk away and then nothing happens. Sometimes we need to ask clarifying questions in the conversation so that we know what answer we are truly getting.

2. **Recognize that highly emotional responses to a request from you may have different root causes.** When someone gets angry, hurt or silent in response to something we've asked it can generally mean one of three things: they're genuinely surprised or shocked and are having an emotional reaction; they are overwhelmed by this news on top of other things going on in their lives; they are utilizing an emotional tactic to make you go away. Your goal is to remain calm and confident, regardless of their response to you.[40]

3. **Ask clarifying, listening questions to make sure you understand.** I love Covey's Habit 5: Seek first to understand, then to be understood. In the heat of the conversation, it may feel counterintuitive to step aside from your goal—your influencing target—to listen for understanding, but it's really important because it demonstrates high levels of the Core Dimensions and helps inform you in the exchange.

Step 4: Choose Your Response

There are a myriad of options at this point in the sequence, which is why we call it Influencing Options®! Remember that generally in an organization, you have two kinds of power to use:

1. **Personal Power**: based on trust and your relationships. Effective especially over time.
2. **Position Power**: granted by the authority of your position. Effective primarily for emergency/crisis or last resort.

Here's a short summary of some of the options once you have determined whether you got a clear "yes" or "no" to your request in Step 2:

If you got a "yes,"

1. You can say, "thank you," and plan to follow-up later.

2. You can say, "thank you," and follow up now with a more detailed formal or informal action plan to help create a behavioral commitment to the verbal "yes."

---

40   See the Three P's for Remaining Calm and Confident in Chapter 7.

If you got a "no,"[41]

1. You can continue to **influence**. Here you have many choices, including using increased control (i.e. Position Power), Negotiation, Negative Natural Consequences, and Confrontation.
2. You can **accept** the "no," and let it go. Sometimes, once you are in the conversation, you realize it's not what you really want, or it's not creating the outcome you want and you decide to move on and let it go. A "letting go" option also might include: doing it yourself, getting someone else to do it or trying again later if the timing is just not right.
3. You can choose **removal**. As mentioned before, this removal can be radical, as in removing yourself entirely (from a job, team or relationship) or you can choose a mini-removal and create specific boundaries or guidelines that will have minimum negative impact to you.

Step 5: Evaluate and Assess

Obviously, this sequence is iterative and can be repeated over and over again. You get to this point in the process and you ask yourself these questions:

1. How did this conversation go? Am I happy with the outcome?
2. Have I strengthened or weakened this relationship with this conversation?
3. Do I feel more or less confident about moving forward with this person?
4. What did I learn about myself in this process?

It's almost like an "After Action Review" for the conversation! What worked, what didn't, what will you do again, what will you definitely not do again?

Particular Influencing Conversations

A lot of times, people want to imagine it takes entirely different skill sets to influence different people, based on their position especially and their relationship secondarily. For example, some believe that influencing up is the most challenging of all; some believe they have no power to influence vendors or suppliers or customers. In reality, the person sitting across from you is exactly that: a person. There are dynamics that come into play, for sure, but one thing I feel certain about:

---

41   These "no" options are really the Three Effective Options introduced in Chapter 2.

relationship pretty much trumps anything. The strength of your relationships, the level of trust that you have with those in your Circle of Influence is directly related to how these conversations are going to go.

As you enter into the important conversations with the people who make up your Circle of Influence, there are some general and specific things to keep in mind in the interactions. Here are some elements that might create differentiation among influencing different relationships:

- Context of situation
- Relationship between you and those you are trying to influence, including history and familiarity with or attachment to the issues at hand
- The existing power dynamic, i.e. are you influencing up, down, or across, internally or externally?
- Your skill and experience with delivering high levels of the Core Dimensions, especially Empathy

That's why, when we help people hone these skills, we suggest that they assess the relationship based on two foundational elements: trust and commitment.

Question 1: What's your relationship like with this person? What is your level of trust?

Question 2: Do you have commitment to shared vision and/or goals? Are you "on the same page?"

Following are some general things to consider and keep in mind when you find yourself in these influencing situations:

Influencing Your Subordinates

1. Normally, when influencing anyone, you always have the Three Effective Choices to use when considering your options or if someone says "no" to you. (Influence, Acceptance, Removal) However, when the case is involving performance, and you are formally responsible for managing the performance of someone, you do not get "Acceptance." You cannot "Accept" poor performance because that means you're really not fulfilling your responsibilities. You either need to Influence the employee to improve performance or you need to Remove them.

2. Keep in mind the power dynamic here. You need to create opportunities for open, honest communication among you and your subordinates. Your relationship with your employees is the single biggest leveraging point in an organization, since the relationship between the employee and the immediate supervisor is what influences performance, morale, productivity, employee engagement, etc.

Influencing Your Peers and Colleagues

1. Having a high-trust colleague at work is invaluable. Cultivate these relationships and develop them. When you need to confront or influence a peer, keep in mind that "saving face" may be incredibly important to them. Be conscientious of where you might have conversations and keep confidential, if possible.

2. Work to create win-wins if a peer or colleague is creating a roadblock or not performing to standard. Confront and discuss directly rather than borrowing Position Power and going above someone's head.

Influencing your Superiors

1. Influencing up is necessary! One essential thing to try to keep in mind in influencing with this power dynamic is that this person's focus is most likely very different from yours. The mistake people often make is that they feel like when they want to influence they really have to build a strong case and so they spend the whole time focusing on themselves. Really appeal to the WIIFM factor: what does this person care about? What's important to him/her in this scenario?

2. You can influence someone to stop micromanaging you! Your language use is critical: ask them for what you want, which is increased autonomy. And, focus on how allowing you more space or authority will benefit them. Offer reassurance that you'll keep them in the loop so they won't be surprised by anything. Again, their reputation, how others see them as leaders and their credibility are probably important to them. They generally like to be seen as competent, confident and carrying out the mission of the organization. Use alignment to help you.

Influencing Boards or Governing Groups

1. Depending upon your direct relationship with a board (or members on a board) you will want to remember that their scope of responsibility and charge is different from yours. If you are the CEO, president or director, the dynamic is such that they may support or not support you as a group, but the group is made up of individuals. Cultivate relationships with individual people. Also, really do the work of Chapter 2, in defining your voice, as your public persona, speaking skills and ability to articulate and present your ideas will set the tone for your relationships here.

2. If you are working with agencies or governing bodies (such as councils, departments, etc.) made up of elected officials, this can cause a complex dynamic, as well. Again, your ability to influence people in this group will be enhanced by having one-one relationships and getting to know and earn the trust of members. It isn't about manipulation or "politics" (even if it is politics), it's about gaining buy-in, commitment, creating common ground and really working to define a win-win scenario.

Influencing Customers and Clients

1. If you take time to develop relationships with customers and clients, they will not only be satisfied (or better yet, delighted), they will be loyal. Relationship-based selling trumps price and the competition almost all the time. There are exceptions, but not many. Your customers will buy from you because they believe you have great value for a reasonable price. Try not to focus on the one-time sale, but rather on the long-term relationship. That will help you create many sales along the way.

2. Most of the time, influencing customers and clients effectively actually involves more listening than talking. If you can discern, through careful listening and clarifying questions (and especially if you do so while delivering high levels of the Core Dimensions), what they really need, you can help them. Don't concentrate on yourself—concentrate on them.

Influencing Vendors, Supplier and Contractors

1. Sometimes, influencing vendors, supplier and contractors is similar to influencing peers because you have tried to establish a collaborative, collegial relationship. One way to positively impact these relationships is by thinking about how you can help their business outside your typical transactions, i.e. referrals, resources or opportunities you hear about, etc.

2. If you have a misunderstanding or a disagreement with a vendor, supplier or contractor, it's really important to confront and resolve respectfully. They are in your network of "success" partners and you want to make sure that you develop strong ties. If it's not a good relationship, and you choose "Removal" you take the high road always, and cut ties expeditiously and respectfully.

What does Chapter 8 have to do with building a Profit Culture?

Your ability to use language well, to enter into conversations boldly and confidently, your ability to create strong relationships and demonstrate understanding will absolutely determine your ability to create, sustain and maintain a Profit Culture.

Chapter 9

The Hidden Costs of Short-Term Compliance Beyond "Because I said so . . . "

Compliance or Commitment?

Sometimes, as leaders, when we take a look at the kind of discipline and commitment it takes to build and sustain a Profit Culture, we just think it's a *lot* of work, a *lot* of effort, and it seems like it will require Herculean effort to pull it off. Where are the good 'ole days when bosses were bosses and everyone else was a pipsqueak?

Is it better to push our people? Challenge them to move lock-step toward the vision? Won't they slack off if we're not driving them, all the time? Isn't it better to light a fire under them than to be too soft in our approach?

First, remember the balancing of accountability and respect in Chapter 1. We know that this isn't an either-or dichotomy. Second, fear *is* a motivator, but not the kind that will influence performance in the way we want for the long term. Examine Figure 9.0 to see the relationship between different types of stress and performance:

We don't want "no stress," because people are apathetic and disengaged, but we don't want extreme stress because that causes people to freeze and take cover—protect themselves. We want the tension created, the **eustress**, to generate enough challenge that people will take pride in their work, feel compelled to push themselves in productive ways, but not push them over the edge.

In a recent study[42] conducted by Green Peak Partners and Cornell, researchers found that conventional wisdom about what sorts of leadership behaviors drive bottom-line results proves to be wrong. Specific findings included:

---

42   "When It Comes to Business Leadership, Nice Guys Finish First: A Green Peak Partners Study Shows that Conventional Wisdom is Wrong—and that Leaders Who Possess Strong Soft Skills Perform Better at Driving Hard Results." J.P. Flaum, MBA. 2009. www.greenpeakpartners.com

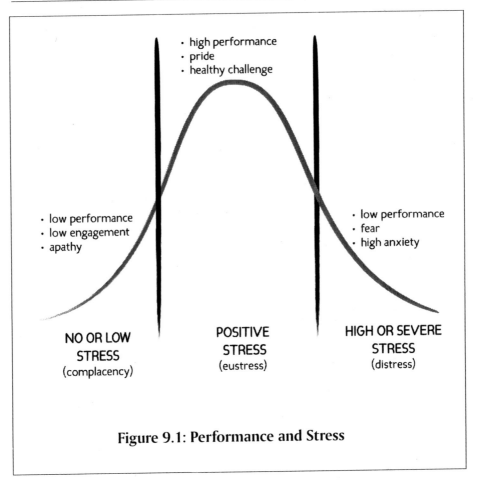

Figure 9.1: Performance and Stress

- "Bully" traits that are often seen as part of a business-building culture were typically signs of incompetence and lack of strategic intellect.
- Poor interpersonal skills lead to under-performance in most executive functions.
- Leadership searches give short shrift to "self-awareness," which should actually be a top criterion.

We know, from examination and application of the Core Dimensions, why this is probably true, and it also just seems so obvious, doesn't it? We know this about leading, and yet, often, we choose short-term compliance over long-term commitment. Why?

When we examine the principle that people follow for one of two reasons—have to or want to—we know that the consequences of establishing one predominant leadership practice over another means that we may get a Compliance Culture, when people are following because they have to, or we are more likely to get a Commitment Culture, when they follow because they want to.

Many of the leaders I meet are, frankly, too busy to think much about creating a Commitment Culture even though they would like to have one. It seems obvious—why wouldn't you want a Commitment Culture? How would you know if you had one? Here are some indicators:

- Low turnover
- High levels of innovation and creativity
- Resilience and sustainability in tough times
- Good levels of stress, i.e. eustress
- Promotion from within the ranks

With all of the possible, good consequences of a Commitment Culture, including the potential for positively impacting the profit of your business, why might leaders choose a Compliance Culture instead? How would you know if you have a Compliance Culture? Here are some indicators:

- Lack of initiative or drive; people seem to be doing the "same old, same old" in their work days
- People wait to be told what to do
- Presence of fear or reluctance to "do the right thing"
- Higher turnover
- Presence of the "walking retired"
- Complaining, negativity, gossip and interpersonal strife
- High burnout

In my experience, organizations and teams only choose a Compliance Culture *by default*—they don't really want one, they just want things to happen quickly, with little fuss, so they can move on to the next thing.

Review Figure 9.2. Where do you plot your current business, organization or team?

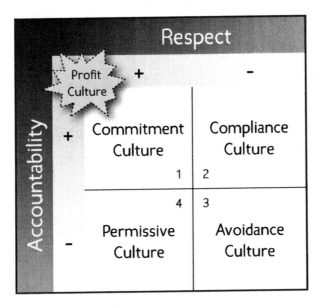

Quadrant 1 - High Respect/High Accountability creates a high commitment culture to support higher profits – engaged high performance, loyalty, trust, innovation and autonomy.

Quadrant 2 - High Accountability/Low Respect creates a compliance culture dependent upon high direction. Low probability for innovation & creativity.

Quadrant 3 - Low Accountability/Low Respect creates an avoidance culture characterized by lack of direction, initiative and loyalty.

Quadrant 4 - High Respect/Low Accountability creates inconsistent performance, missed opportunities and eventual disengagement.

Figure 9.2: Accountability and Respect: Culture Implications

In Real Life:

For several years, I have worked with professionals in law enforcement, corrections and emergency services. Their business is based on a paramilitary structure and processes which value chain-of-command and the use of position power. They know how to respond and deal with emergencies and crises, which is their business, and we are happy they know how to do so! However, even they are not in emergency-mode 24/7—there are down times, maintenance times, and long shifts with no incidents whatsoever. Yet, often, the least progressive of these agencies default to the use of position power over and over, which creates, in the long run, a Compliance Culture, including many characteristics in the list above. They can be masterful at giving orders and directives. Modern businesses, large and small, often default to the use of position power, too, because they think it will take less time to just simply order someone to do something. In other words, I use my power of my position to tell you what to do, limiting your choices, and thus getting what I want more quickly. The problem here is that we get only short-term results, which is what we may need in an actual emergency but works against us in the regular day-to-day operations of meeting our business objectives.

Position Power vs. Personal Power

Basically, when you are influencing as a leader, you have two kinds of power you can use to influence: position power and personal power.

Position Power and Personal Power

Position Power	Personal Power
Granted to you via the authority of your position—you're the boss!	Based on the strength of your relationship and trust building skills
Essential to use in emergency or crisis situations where discussion and consensus may take too much time to respond	Correlates with your delivery of the Core Dimensions (Respect, Empathy, Specificity and Genuineness) and creates an environment that supports high levels of productivity, trust, morale
Essential to use as a last resort or final option when you have utilized all other options to create movement, such as in improving performance	Typically makes it easier to influence the same person or group when you return for another influencing scenario

It is important to note that using Position Power or Personal Power is neither right nor wrong, you just want to be aware of which type of power you are using to influence, what sort of patterns of behaviors you are creating using your power, and what the long-term objectives are for creating a Profit Culture.

Hidden Cost #1: It's inefficient—it takes more time to lead this way.

This often feels counter-intuitive to many leaders, but a quick order or directive actually becomes inefficient over time as a leadership and influencing practice. Why does it take more time to lead this way? First, when we are influencing subordinates or employees, and we have created a Compliance Culture dependent upon the use of position power to influence and get things done, we create a culture of waiters . . . not carrying trays of Bellinis for brunch, sadly, but rather people who are waiting around for us to tell them what to do. Therefore, like waiters I used to work with, they're hiding out in the back station until a table is seated for them rather than acting on their own volition. My old manager use to say, "if you have time to lean, you have time to clean," and though this isn't exactly what you may be facing with your employees, the same idea applies: if you have essentially trained your people to wait for your order or directive, they will.

Nowadays, over and over, I hear leaders express dismay at the time they suspect their employees are surfing the Internet or ordering sweaters online while they are supposed to be "working." One of the places I'd look first is to see if you've created a culture where they are simply waiting for you to tell them what to do because they are used to it. One thing we used to say when creating structured on-the-job training programs (OJT) was that when an employee walks in for his first day of work, he is learning . . . he is being trained, in essence, to navigate the new job terrain. If we pay attention to how we structure and foster the learning environment, then he will learn what we want him to learn about working at our company or on our team. If we either create a culture of dependence by using only position power to influence, or we leave his learning up to chance . . . we get what we get!

When someone waits for direction from us, this often necessitates multiple conversations, and often more follow-up, checking in, and managing. Often, leaders who have fallen into the habit of defaulting to using position power to influence become micro-managers. It's a downward spiral that no one other than the greatest of control-freaks admits to liking: seriously, who has *time* for micromanaging? Yet, when we, through our own good intentions, imagine that using a quick shot of position power to give a directive will get the work done more quickly, we create a messy web of confusion where we have to go back again and again to make sure things get done—so that what we've tried to influence will come to fruition.

Now, don't confuse this with the communication required to effectively delegate and/or assign work. You can use your Personal Power (much discussed in Chapters 3, 4 and 9) to both delegate and assign work, thus preventing that culture of waiters mentioned above. In fact, the biggest difference in delegating and assigning work is in the efforts we must provide in supervision and how much time it takes to do so.

Delegating and Assigning

Delegating	Assigning
Higher level of trust; you are confident in the completion and quality	May be a new task or project; they are less experienced
You identify the outcome or result, but you give them autonomy on the process of how they get there	You identify the outcome or result and make suggestions or list requirements for the process
Identify timeline/timeframe	You have regularly scheduled check-ins, benchmarks or communication throughout
Be available as a resource, but they initiate the contact with you	You drive most of the communication during the process

Don't be confused about assigning work as equal to micromanaging—one of the ultimate sins of supervision and management—everyone hates this! Micromanaging is about a lack of trust, not about using too much power or providing enough direction. Sometimes, we engage in Mirage Delegation, too. This is where we say we're delegating, and we may even act like it initially, but then we keep showing up, messing about, and getting in the middle of the work. We've not really turned over the reins! [43]

Examine Figure 9.3. When you think about the people on your team, where do you plot your Delegation Diagnostic?

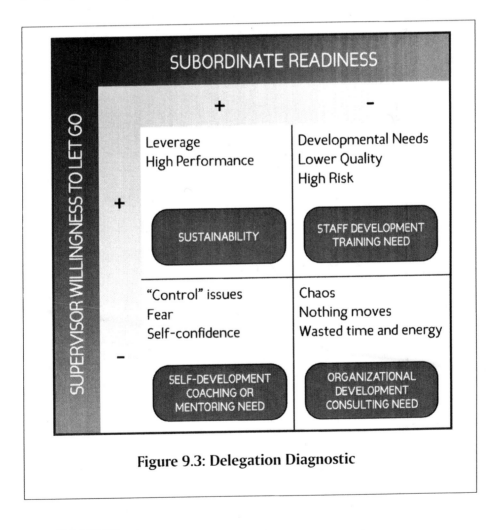

Figure 9.3: Delegation Diagnostic

---

43   Credit goes to Jeff Shimizu from Philips for coining "Mirage Delegation."

Another reason that influencing this way takes more time is that those who *want* to do well, please you, get on the bus (or whatever) will hesitate and avoid the risk that they might do the wrong thing. You have created, by virtue of the directive, a dependency, and therefore they do not trust themselves to make the right decisions within the boundaries or guidelines of the mission and vision of your organization or team. It's better just to wait, to see what you want, than to take the risk of doing it wrong, so they don't. And, meanwhile, you're not even thinking about this, putting out fires and responding to so-called emergencies, so time that could be spent in their action and commitment to creating movement toward the goal, and higher profits, is stalled-out or stuck, until you have that next conversation, drive-by, or one-on-one.

Hidden Cost #2: You stifle creativity, innovation and autonomy

Defaulting to Position Power as a habit doesn't mean you are always barking orders or yelling at your people. Very nice people with softer styles or charming dispositions can create a Compliance Culture without taking on the persona of a sergeant major. It's sneaky that way. In addition to creating a culture of waiters who don't create their own initiatives or act of their own volition, one of the worst things that a Compliance Culture can do is stifle creativity, innovation, and autonomy.

Who cares about creativity and innovation? Most of the companies I work for and with do—in fact, many will posit the assertion "innovate or die," especially in high-tech fields, highly competitive industries, or CPG firms committed to capturing higher market share. Consumers are addicted to the latest and greatest, we are growth-oriented and only the boundaries of imagination create the current limitations on innovation and creativity. Human nature plays a role, too, and when a work environment is supported by delivering high levels of the Core Dimensions (Respect, Empathy, Specificity and Genuineness) you can create a fertile ground for growth, innovation and creativity. On the other hand, if via your highly directive influencing style and overuse of Position Power, you are contributing to an environment where lower levels of Respect, Empathy, Specificity and Genuineness abound, people are cordoning themselves off in silos or hiding under their desks, either literally or figuratively. In the corrections industry, they'd say, "do your eight and hit the gate." In other words, Compliance Cultures create space for the minimum, run-of-the-mill routine work to be done (only when you ask, of course) and there's no impetus to do anything out of the ordinary and especially nothing extraordinary.

Capitalizing on Strengths and Talent

Much has been written in the past fifteen years about creating strengths-based[44] cultures and hiring for talent in organizations. Over and over again, the research supports that when you have your employees' talents and strengths aligned with the organizational mission and vision, you've got the perfect opportunity for alignment leading to higher profits. In other words, if I get to do what I do best, and what I like to do, and I get to meet the mission of my organization and fulfill the expectations of my job, the news is pretty good! However, relying on a Compliance Culture means that you're not tapping into my strengths because you're highly likely to be giving me directives, rather than having two-way conversations, and therefore, you see only the skills needed for the task at-hand. Here's an example that exemplifies an opportunity that created a great pay-off for all involved:

In Real Life

A non-profit who regularly conducted fundraising campaigns had multiple databases in multiple divisions of the organization creating missed opportunities, doubling-up of work, and inefficiencies overall. No one person could access data for donors and volunteers easily. An intern had been hired to work in the program office to help with administrative support tasks. Luckily, because her manager engaged her using her Personal Power, interacting in two-way conversation, sharing ideas and listening, the intern was able not only to teach herself a complex data program, but also to collect and organize data from across the organization. This created a tool for the organization to use for many years to come, and improved the ability to gather, sort and organize data. If her manager had just directed her to stuff envelopes and sort files (which she did as well), there's a good chance that none of the positive consequences would've occurred, including the engagement of talent, a savings of resources, and an increase in efficiency. Everyone was happy at the outcome!

---

44   Especially the work of Donald Clifton in Soar With Your Strengths and Marcus Buckingham's *First, Break All the Rules* and the subsequent "strengths" books and research.

Another example suggests that when we create dependencies based on a Compliance Culture, we may not even know what sorts of talents and skills we have available to us in our organizations:

In Real Life

One senior-level leader in a high tech firm shared with me his dismay that he really didn't have any "bench strength" among his middle managers—no one to take on the leading of the larger, strategic teams and carry the organization into the future. "No one is stepping forward," he'd say, concerned that his direct reports had not adequately prepared their employees for promotion and advancement. Although there certainly could've been gaps in talent and skill, I always want to examine whether there might be some obstacles in the way of these middle managers rising to become high performing stars. Indeed, after further investigation, it seems that the environment itself, low in trust and morale, competitive among teams, and highly directive, had masked the talent of these middle managers. They were afraid of stepping out, doing the wrong thing, or coming up with creative, innovative ways to solve the organization's problems, so they didn't. Many were playing it safe, cruising under the radar, hoping to wait out this leadership's initiatives so they could put their time in and hopefully transfer or gain the experience they needed to move on. It wasn't until the leaders began to improve their delegation and establish higher levels of communication and action based on the Core Dimensions, that leaders began to emerge from the ranks for promotion and advancement.

Avoiding Malicious Compliance

I'm not sure which is worse, or more costly—a fear-based culture where you are not tapping into the talents and skills you have available, or an environment where employees are actively disengaged, or even falling into the trap of "malicious compliance." I always imagine that no one but the direst of government bureaucracies and staid organizations suffer the consequences of malicious compliance, but I must report that it exists at every level, in just about every kind of business. What this means is that you have people who are doing their jobs (barely or minimally) but who are so disengaged they create distractions and disruptions for others via gossip, negativity, rumor-mongering or sabotaging. Because they are not fully engaged in their own work, committed to the mission of your organization, they lack focus on the work itself. An overuse of position power may not be the only cause of this, but it is one important place to look. When people are creatively engaged because you have fostered strong, Personal-Power based relationships, they don't have time to engage in anti-social, negative behaviors.

Gaining Market Edge

Gaining a competitive edge in your market, regardless of the industry, depends upon your ability to respond to trends, make good decisions about shifting business direction, and a willingness to challenge the status quo. Often, it's your designers, engineers, practitioners and those close to the work of your work who can and need to come up with these innovative and creative ways to gain a market edge. Or, they need to work alongside the researchers who study market trends and innovations to utilize the data which can help them set some parameters around how to push the conventions and imagine the next, best thing for your products and services. When we've created waiters, short-term compliance operators or those who are minimally engaged their thoughts tend toward *who cares about the market, unless it serves my own, individual ego needs? Besides, there's no particular pay-off for me to put myself out there because you're going to tell me what to do anyway.*

Hidden Cost #3: Lack of Loyalty

It may seem strange to imagine that the overuse of position power, or a compliance culture, could impact employee loyalty, but it does. When you have a loyal contingent:

- People give you the benefit of the doubt
- People give the company the benefit of the doubt
- People weather tough conditions and difficult change
- People want to do the right thing, and create ways of saying "yes" to serving customers better
- People want to save you money, make you money, or both

Turnover

Without loyalty, you're at greater risk for employees leaving. Employee turnover is very costly. Actual dollar amounts vary, but consistently reports confirm that on average you can expect to expend 1.5 times (or 150%) of that person's salary to replace him or her. That sales rep who makes about $65,000? Expect the replacement costs to be $97,500. Executive level employee at $120,000? Cost to replace: $180,000. Even if we're talking an hourly employee with minimal specific skills at $35,000 per year, that's still going to cost you $52,500. Multiply these by the people you're losing each year and that will give you an idea about how this is affecting your profits. Turnover deceptively eats away at the margins because it's tough to calculate time lost in searching for someone new, time to get someone up to speed and producing, as well as time others are distracted from the loss/gain of a new person on the team. Even if you think you can afford this, if you're trying to improve your Profit Culture, you can't ignore the impact that this can have on the bottom line. The best things to do to prevent turnover and increase loyalty?

- Hire for talent and hire well
- Set specific, clear expectations
- Clear the swamp[45]
- Engage their hearts and minds.

Resilience

One of my favorite resources to share with leaders is Patrick Lencioni's book *Overcoming the Five Dysfunctions of a Team*. He's got a great model for potential dysfunctions[46] that demonstrates the significance of trust as the foundation for eventually gaining the results you desire. One notion I gleaned from his work is that there's a significant difference between a highly functioning team and one that struggles, especially when faced with change or chaos: the highly functioning team quickly gets back on track, while the struggling team gets distracted, suffers from conflict or interpersonal strife and dips in performance. In other words, these high-functioning teams have resilience.

This is applicable when we think about influencing, as well, and especially using Position Power versus Personal Power. Cultivating resilience allows us to weather difficult times, changes in the economy or market, the coming and going of employees due to promotion or turnover. When you have cultivated loyalty via

---

45   More about Clearing the Swamp in Chapter 5.
46   Lack of trust, lack of ability to deal with conflict, lack of commitment, lack of accountability and lack of results.

the development of strong relationships, and especially through the use of Personal Power, people will stay. They will give you and your organization the benefit of the doubt. They will be willing to be more patient, to dive in and help when needed, to believe that things will get better, move forward, resume. When we create dependencies in our Compliance Cultures, we abort the qualities for resilience and instead create a foundation for instability and inconsistency in the face of change.

Loss of Intellectual Capital

Another hidden cost of a lack of loyalty in a Compliance Culture is that when someone actually leaves, or they "leave" on the job, your organization suffers from losing the knowledge that that person carries with him or her. Two things can happen, either they lack a willingness to share this information because they don't want to, or they never get to create it in the first place because of the directive nature of your communication with them. In other words, since much of the value of an organization lies in its knowledge—both explicit and tacit, when we are not regularly cultivating or mining this knowledge, there's a great chance we lose it---when an employee leaves—or we never even get to it because we've stifled creativity and innovation, and, on top of that, they feel no particular loyalty to just simply come forward with it. For example, when employees are highly engaged in a Commitment Culture, they regularly think of ways to make the business better because they are empowered to do so, or they will try to capture a process, an idea or a system that they are creating or developing. The passivity of a Compliance Culture runs counter to this type of pro-active communication and activity.

KEY POINT

What does Chapter 9 have to do with building a Profit Culture?

A Commitment Culture, with a good balance of accountability and respect via leaders and a solid consistent delivery of the Core Dimensions, *is* a Profit Culture.

Chapter 10

A Transformational Workplace: Committing to and Sustaining a Profit Culture

Where Do We Go From Here?

Now what?

> ### In Real Life
>
> *Recently, I was visiting a client in Atlanta with whom I have been working for the past 18 months. They are doing good work, recommitting to their Team Agreements, utilizing their talents, taking risks in unchartered waters. We were noting the progress they had made, the efforts, and the parts that had gotten messy. Some are reluctantly hopeful; some are completely all-in. It is almost time, as their consultant and advisor, for me to go. "In the end," I shared with them, "the goal is for you to become emancipated from me!" We all laughed, but this is true. This disengagement is important in our process because I am external to the organization; they must carry on and do the work they've created and begun, and I feel confident they can.*

A lot of times when we begin a culture change project, people want some assurances. They want to know whether the time, effort and resources will have a big ROI[46] and how they will sustain this shift they've begun. They ask because they've seen initiatives come and go, they begin the journeys hopeful and helpful and they want to see sustainability, and sometimes, it doesn't work. Sometimes, the gravitational pull back to the old ways of thinking and doing seem to override the enthusiasm and initial belief that they can not only bring about change but also continue to implement and execute the new habits and behaviors. They want some guarantees. There are no guarantees—the only way that you, as a leader in a Profit Culture, can create increased probability of long-term change is to commit wholeheartedly to do your best, to be willing to make the internal shifts necessary, to call into question when something seems amiss. Remember, it is the emotional fortitude of the leader and a communication infrastructure that will make or break your initiative. It's your play—you've got to direct it.

Here in this last chapter, I'd like to offer some insights for you to consider as you examine how you might commit to, influence, and sustain a Profit Culture, and why you might want to invest the effort and resources to do so. The idea here is to discuss what follows not only *after* you've done the work of the previous chapters, but also *as* you continue to do the work of leading. Each is its own topic (book, really) and the intent is to allow you some rumination for what might be next for you, your organization, and the people in it. My current favorite resources are cited at the end.

Dealing with or Creating Great Change

Let's just say that change is inevitable. Let's say that change is irrefutable. There is a whole genre of writing and postulations about "change management," which seems, with each passing month, to be less of an oxymoron than I originally thought. Heraclitus was right: "No man ever steps in the same river twice, for it's not the same river and he's not the same man." When I ran my first Danskin triathlon, their tag line was, "The woman who starts the race is not the same woman who finishes the race." We are both transformed by change and we transform those events and organizations with which we interconnect in that change. As a leader, we can say the same about you: once you begin the journey to building a Profit Culture and becoming *that* leader, you and your organization are forever changed.

This is a good thing. Remember that a *Profit Culture is any organizational culture of abundance where people are engaged in growth-related activities to support the economic*

---

46   Return on Investment. We didn't even know this term in poetry school!

interchange. Just by definition we know change is at the core of this dynamic—growth involves the whole of the life process: the germination of a seed idea, the planting, the cultivation, the tending, the harvest, the celebration of your labor, the decay and composting, enriched and fertile soil—the cycle repeats. All of the people in an organization take some part in this process, some may come and go, some will see the cycle through years of progression.

How, then, can you sustain any good work that you've invested? If everything will eventually change, why not just ride the tide and see how it goes? *You can*, of course, but most leaders are called to be leaders because they'd like to lead from the front, cultivate and foster this growth, rather than simply forage for what they might find or what's left over.

Dealing with Change

Why do we persist in thinking things won't change? Perhaps it is human nature to believe that when we step out of the bed in the morning, the floor will be there, sturdy as ever, so that we can fumble our way to the kitchen to turn the kettle on. That seems like a pretty safe assumption, doesn't it? Certainly, for many years, we could have assumed that our daily lives would be, for the most part, the same—we'd rise early with the sun, tend to our chores and our plots of land, help our children grow, watch the sun set on the horizon. In fact, prior to the Industrial Revolution, our lives—in terms of economic, social or occupational status—did not change significantly from year to year or even generation to generation.

But, all this changed, of course. And, if we're honest, it was always changing; no matter the almanac considered, there was always the weather we couldn't perfectly predict! It is the *pace* of change in current times that has us spooked. It is in our ability to respond to the new day beyond the trek to the kitchen coffee pot that has us cranky. In fact, we really don't hate change at all; we just don't like feeling as if we have no say in it. Think about it: if you wanted to change something, like your hairstyle, the color of your living room walls, or your city of residence, you'd just do it. You'd change in a snap and be happy about it! Our challenge is that some changes require strategy and contingency planning. But mostly, if we think the change is going to be for the better, we're all about moving forward with it. It's when we feel like we are *being* changed; we are the passive recipients or victims of change, which makes us unhappy.

Resistance

Generally, I see three main reasons for resisting to change:

Fear. This is number one for a reason. Primarily, fear of the unknown and fear of loss are some of the first indications of resistance. Even if the change is for the better, it's going to be different, and we don't know how to deal with different yet, so we'd rather have this old thing we know about. At least we know about it! Or, we fear losing status, routines, co-workers, responsibilities, etc. We become attached to people and routines and we create our perceptions of the way things are around their consistency. If we lose those familiar things, now what do we do?

Resentment. This could be a close cousin to fear, but it begins to manifest itself in behaviors or attitudes toward the change. It can specifically be directed at the person(s) instituting the change, like a new boss or supervisor, or it can be more globally directed, as in "the government" or "headquarters" or "Administration." So, instead of responding to whether the change itself is for the better, the resentment is focused specifically on the change agent, i.e. kill the messenger.

Disagreement. Sometimes we're not afraid and we're not resentful, we just believe the change is wrong! We think whoever made this crazy decision is hanging out in the ozone, hasn't thought it through, or has become disconnected from the real work. It's just a stupid decision and worthy of complaining, moaning and lost time of productivity. What's almost worse is when this disagreement response is perpetuated by a lack of information; it can lead to apathy and malicious compliance.

How can you help impact the quality of the change process?

Information. In my experience with clients, teams and leaders, this is the number one issue—the perception of a lack of information as it relates to the daily workings of an organization. Here's my suggestion: share all the information you can. Make it readily available in a variety of forms or forums. Give everyone an opportunity to know the specifics of the change, anticipated timelines, and expectations. Err on the side of more information rather than less, and if some information is confidential or sacrosanct, tell them you can't tell them all the information right now. Be honest.

Inclusion. I'll start right up front with a caveat: don't do it unless you mean it. When you can include employees in the decision-making process about the changes to occur, it creates a smoother path for buy-in to the change and therefore less resistance. Sometimes, because of timeliness, nature of the proposed change, etc. inclusion is not possible or practical. Shared governance is a lovely idea, but not everyone needs to be in on the conversation about compensation packages or which toilet paper to put in the restrooms—it's not a prudent use of people's time to be in on every decision. However, if you examine the big picture of the situation and you decide that participation in the discussion, or a survey, or another query of some kind would benefit the change process, do it. However, don't institute an exercise of inclusion and then ignore the feedback. This doesn't mean that you have to include every crazy idea, but you can create a way to value input and respond with logic and effectiveness aligned with your mission. Think long-term. Think about the next change when you'll try to gain buy-in again.

Follow up. This is the ongoing practice of sharing and receiving information. Create a way to gather feedback during the change process. Create a way to respond to feedback. Communicate in person, in writing, in groups—any way to assist people to adapt while minimizing fear, resentment and disagreement. If you don't follow up, you're simply setting yourself up for resistance again.

I often remind people of their Three Effective Choices.[47] Most often, it is the way we perceive change that steers us in our responses. If we see change as a learning opportunity, a challenge or a way to know something different about ourselves, we can feel confident that we can deal with it, even if it wasn't our idea. We always have three choices!

Balancing the Numbers and the People: Performance Management

Performance management[48], as a topic to support Profit Cultures, is really its own book! Here, though, are some important things to note as you look for your next steps in sustaining your changes. First, there are three common myths associated with Performance Management:

Myth 1: managing performance is something done in isolation and it is the responsibility only of the immediate supervisor.

Myth 2: managing performance happens during the yearly evaluation.

---

47   Influence, Acceptance or Removal.
48   You can go to www.libbywagner.com, however, and check out the Special Reports for one specifically devoted to Performance Management and the Six Keys to Managing Performance.

Myth 3: managing performance is primarily focused on the technical skills, i.e. "hard skills" of the job.

Instead, consider the following:

1. Managing performance is part of an overall organizational system.

Often, people who care about managing performance see it as an isolated thing they have to do *to* the people who work for them, such as thinking that they have to deal with people issues or complete an annual evaluation or appraisal. Certainly, these activities are part of managing performance, but the employees of an organization, and their performance, actually drive what happens in the organization. Managing performance is so critical to the success of an organization and so costly if it is done poorly. When an organizational system is in alignment, every person's role, every decision that is made, is tied to the overall strategy and mission of the organization. I can tell you how what I do, no matter my job, contributes to the goals, whether related to service, profits, products or processes. It is easy to see how one action or reaction affects every other part of the system. Without system alignment, there is a high probability for ineffective and inefficient things to happen, whether it's how you spend your resources or what direction you want to lead your organization or team. It's more effective if everything is lined up and connected purposefully rather than simply organically.

2. Managing performance is both a process and an end result.

Too many leaders and organizations want to rely on the end-of-the-year evaluation or appraisal to manage performance. This is both ineffective and risky. When employees are empowered to take part in the performance process through consistent feedback, ongoing coaching, and opportunities for development and growth, managing performance becomes a partnership between the manager and the employee rather than an action performed upon the employee every December or at an anniversary date. The margin for error—the gaps in time where performance can keep moving swiftly down the wrong track—is significant. When you only talk about performance once a year, many employees make the incorrect assumption that "no news is good news," and are surprised to find out in their performance appraisal that someone is not happy with their performance or that corrections need to be made. An ongoing, proactive strategy for managing performance allows employees to correct and adjust performance along the way and to keep building on the positive practices and good skills they may have.

3. If it's affecting performance positively or negatively, it's job-related

You should create performance expectations for both the technical skills of the job, or those related to expertise, experience and content, and the interpersonal skills necessary for the job, such as teamwork, collaboration, problem-solving and decision-making. If you can define it behaviorally and set criteria, you can hold them accountable for it.

Managing Morale and Engagement

Certainly much of the content of this whole book is about managing morale and engagement, since a high-morale, highly engaged workforce is much more likely to help you foster and sustain a Profit Culture. What is morale? What can we do about it?

If morale is the ability of people to maintain belief in an organization or institution, then whose responsibility is it to see that morale is managed? What happens when morale sinks or stinks? Some studies suggest that morale actually has two parts-response and focus. When someone feels good about her work and believes in her organization, she is willing to respond appropriately to her tasks or duties. She is also able to focus on those tasks or duties with minimal distractions from her feelings about her work because she believes in what she's doing and what her organization is doing. Consider all the components to this foundation of organizational morale:

First, the organization needs to have something in which people can believe—this is usually a service or purpose identified by the organizational Vision/Mission. Second, she needs to know her place, her part in this mission and what she's responsible for contributing. Third, she needs regular feedback and praise to help keep her on track and on target. All of these contribute to the internal work, the intrinsic commitment to an organization's mission or vision, but the important thing is that they directly impact what happens on the outside—the external manifestations of this belief that what she's doing is worth it. Often, people may believe in a particular work group or office unit with whom they work closely—their team—but they do not believe in the larger organization or in the organization's leaders. They stay and try to do their best in their work group because they are committed to those people and those tasks or outcomes. However, without a commitment to the organization itself, they are also more likely to falsely represent the organization or to behave unethically. What we need is a commitment to a shared goal, which is why organizational alignment is so important.

Healthy assessment

Healthy organizations assess themselves. They aren't afraid to ask the questions, and the recognize when administering an employee engagement survey (sometimes called employee satisfaction), no matter the results, it's an opportunity to learn. Assessments like these (and the one we walked through in Clear the Swamp) are ways to check perception and ways to check the pulse of an organization. The biggest mistake organizations make *if* they measure employee engagement is either not responding at all, or responding only partially, It has the same effect as a Team Agreement or Clear the Swamp with no follow-up: damaged credibility of leadership, a sense that you wasted their time, and generally an unwillingness to participate again because they don't see that it makes a difference.

I think it's important, also, not to fall into the trap of what some educational institutions do—teach to the test. In other words, if you gather data that seems negative or problematic, do respond, do try to investigate and make changes if necessary. However, if your efforts are not executed sincerely, employees will know and they will be suspicious of any changes you are trying to make because of the lack of sincerity. This creates resistance, which just fuels low morale again.[49]

Sharing responsibility

Indeed, morale is an organizational responsibility, but you are the leader. You are out front. If you're not getting the kind of enthusiastic, committed employee behaviors you want, the first place you need to investigate is you. Are you consistently modeling the behaviors you want to see? Are you leading by example? And, are you asking for what you want, while delivering high levels of the Core Dimensions? Morale is, at the bottom line, your responsibility as a leader. All of the tools contained in this book will help you make the shifts you desire so that you can empower those who

---

49   I just love *The Carrot Principle* by Chester Elton and Adrian Gostick. They've got a great, research-backed resource for how to successfully utilize recognition and reward to positively impact a workplace and its results.

work for you to recognize that they, too, are empowered to impact morale—they are not victims of it.

Tough Times

At the writing of this book, we are certainly on the upswing of recovery, but the past few years have been a struggle for many companies. Truth be told, the biggest test of your leadership is actually when things *aren't* going well—when you are facing some tough times and big challenges. This is the crucible for making the harder metals we need to carry on in better times.

What to do as a leader when faced with gray skies?

Maintain Perspective. There are always a lot of doomsdayers and naysayers out there. Sometimes they mask themselves in the dark cloaks of cynicism and "I'm just being real" behaviors. Don't buy into it. Choose carefully those you spend time with, listen to and take to heart. Try to remember that underneath the dark cloak is fear of disappointment — cynicism is sure paralysis for organizations and people. If this applies to you, consider carefully: perhaps for now you might give up your addiction to information? I know this sounds counter to what I usually preach — learn, grow, develop, improve — but incessant media madness (including print, television and Internet) will dampen your spirits at best and make you paranoid at worst. Focus on what's inside your circle of influence and remember that *you always have the ability to choose* how to respond to what happens to you and around you.

Be Inspiring. If you're leading others, they're always watching you anyway, but they're really watching you now. Talk about scrutiny. Talk about pressure! The interesting thing about inspiring others is that often it happens because we are inspiring ourselves. What creates positive, life-affirming joy for you? Or if that's just too much for a gray, rainy perspective, what gives you and those around you some sense of relief? Spend time on those topics, activities and projects that mean something to you and to your organization or team.

Believe in Your Own Resilience. You will prevail. What's the alternative? If you always have the ability to choose, you can choose something different. Think about times in the past when you made it through a tough or difficult situation? What did you do well? What did you learn? You don't have to know how this will all play out, you just need to stay in the game, and though many have shared with me recently that they just want to "keep their heads down" or be "happy I just have a job," resist that urge and be willing to be strong and stand out in the crowd. It's the best time to do it — it will differentiate you within your organization or among your competitors.

Celebrate Successes, Regardless How Small. One of my clients had to navigate two lay-offs in twelve months. It's painful. It's heart-wrenching and stressful, but the second time, they were better at it. They know what to expect and how to make decisions and treat people well. Along the way, they've improved productivity, communication, and inched along the red/black lines of profitability. Investigate the practice of Appreciative Inquiry and the gentle, yet powerful shift this process can create in an organization and among individuals. Ask on a regular basis: *What's the good news? What can we celebrate? How are we succeeding?*

Transparency

The definition I like to use for transparency is the ability to see through; or the physical property of allowing light to pass through. I know . . . very poetic stretch to discuss telling the truth in organizations or cultivating candor, right? However, the notions of truth, perception, reality, fact and opinion all come into question when we are asking our employees and teammates to be honest, forthright and *transparent*. We want to invite them to illuminate us.

Common Obstacles to Transparency

When I queried an international group of independent consultants, I asked them what they could cite, from their experiences with clients, as reasons why we're not "telling the truth" in organizations as much as we might like to see:

- Self-preservation
- Power and authority
- Fiefdoms or turf
- Credibility
- Exhaustion
- Survival
- Denial
- Fear of retribution
- Clash in values
- Prioritization of values
- History
- Relationships
- Futility—it won't matter

Again, here as a leader, you must lead from the front and be willing to create the kind of environment where people are willing to risk the truth. James O'Toole[50] calls it "telling truth to the top," which we badly need and suffer from when we don't get it. What do you need to cultivate to encourage transparency in your organization?

- *A candid speaker and receptive listener*
  Cultivate two-way conversations without fear of risk or retribution.

- *Find your blind spot*
  Solicit feedback from those who will be willing to tell you if you have any blind spots that are obscuring your vision and getting in the way of full understanding or effectiveness

- *Create honesty opportunities*
  An open-door policy is never enough. The power dynamic is too powerful and those who might really want to be honest and forthright really have to muster a lot of courage to come forward if the issue is serious enough. Create space, time and places for honesty to happen.

- *Remember that "how" matters*
  Barking out, "Does anyone have any questions?" isn't going to solicit the willingness to step out and ask or offer up. How you ask for honesty, respond to it, and deal with it matters if you want to encourage an environment where it can happen with regularity and consistency.

Recommitment: Discipline and Practice

Your own recommitment to your initiatives and culture change is essential, and you cannot do this from a sense of exhaustion, a sense of being overwhelmed or overly burdened. Often, it is from this place where we find the seeds of a need for change or adjustment. It's okay to pay attention to this; I think it's detrimental to let it go on and on. Sometimes you need to behave counter-intuitively to the notion that you must work harder and faster. It will never be manageable like that because "harder" and "faster" isn't the issue. Here are ways I have helped leaders gain perspective and recommit to their good work:

---

50   *Transparency: How Leaders Create a Culture of Candor*, Warren Bennis, Daniel Goleman and James O'Toole, Jossey-Bass, 2008.

The Myth of Balance

One thing I learned long ago as a teacher is that if you're good, you end up developing this sense that the work is never, ever finished, and it can get pretty discouraging. Leaders sometimes feel this way, too. When you are devoted to your ongoing growth and development, your team's development, the innovative initiatives of your organization. Your "to do" list just gets longer and longer. Americans are the worst at this probably—we really do not cultivate and understand the need for holiday and vacation in the truest sense as a culture (otherwise, we wouldn't mete it out like poverty rations from the HR office), and therefore we perpetuate our own exhaustion. But certainly, we are not the only society with a growing sense of unfinished things to be done.

This is why it's especially important to pay attention to a few things: you do not have three, four or six lives. You have one, integrated and interconnected life. Your work, your home, your relationships, your self—all of these need the interplay of the others.[51]

Top 3: Prioritizing

This is completely tactical: pick three things. Each day at the end of my day, I jot down the three most important, pressing things I really want to accomplish or deal with the next day. This allows me to not only manage my time, but to cull out the lesser things or delegate them. There's a psychological benefit to three: you can do more, which is fine, but if you just can get those three done, you will feel a sense of accomplishment and progress, which is important to your psyche.

Leadership Voice exercises

Every so often (I'd say at least once a year), go back and repeat the Leadership Voice exercises in Chapter 2. Allow yourself time for reflection and contemplation. Even if it seems like you can't get away, can't squeeze out the time, do it anyway. The payoffs are huge and allow you to get clear, grounded and affirms you're on track or let's you know you've strayed.

Strategic time

I used to think this plagued entrepreneurs more than business leaders inside organizations, but that's simply not true. The gravitational pull to the organization is into the operations, the weeds, the muddy muck. It's really hard to stay out of it

---

51   See David Whyte's *The Three Marriages*. 2009.

and so it can become a pattern of problem-solving intervention and fire-fighting. I suggest identifying something you can realistically commit to—one hour per week, one half-day a month—a time you devote to strategic thinking, big picture assessment, etc. and you get out of the "weeds" and delegate and assign what you can. You can never make progress if you're down in the trenches all the time because you can't see the far horizon.

Time away

For twelve years, I did not take a true vacation. I had some time to travel to family for some holidays, but I did not take time away. It's hard for me to write that without falling into judging myself harshly for such craziness! Did anyone notice? Did it matter? Was I impressing my bosses or employees? NO! It was some sort of ridiculous martyr behavior or lack of confidence . . . Take time off! Turn off your technology. Focus and be present with the people in your life, an activity you love, a place that inspires you. Tonight it's Artwalk in Pioneer Square, I can hear the live music playing. I'm leaving my office very soon. Time away is important.

Finally

Remember our Profit Culture Pyramid. It's simple, really, based on some common sense principles and practices. Most importantly, it's possible!

We have arrived at the conclusion. I've offered the things I know have worked with my clients to help them create practices, behaviors, and thinking that can not only build a Profit Culture but also sustain one. When it's all said and done, an organization that is flexible, resilient, creative and consistent is able to weather any season, any shifts or stops that might occur. Change is inevitable and even desirable.

I love astrophysicist Saul Perlmutter's sentiment when he was awarded the Carnegie Mellon Dickson Prize for Science: "Your job as a scientist is to figure out how you've been fooling yourself." It's our job as leaders, too. Leading an organization takes energy, effort and discipline. Yet mostly, leading well takes self-awareness. It is as much an inner journey as it is a list of things to do or tips and keys to success. There's no magic bullet or one answer, but I do know this: your ability to create a place and a space where good work can happen will yield the results you want, and even some you haven't yet imagined that you want.

Be willing to be vulnerable, honest and creative. Reflect and assess. Read a poem or two. Hang out with people who inspire you. Creating Profit Cultures is possible and we need great leaders to do it. There's good work to be done.

A poem here for the journey ahead—it's not just that bottom line, the end of the race, the desired results. It is that, and it is also the unexpected joy that being fully present in the process brings.

Poem for March

Today a run along Beach Drive:
the last bit, stretching, breathing,
willing my body to the end spot,
the concentrated effort, the goal, the seen
accomplishment becomes completely consuming.
When a sudden gust of wind, and indeed,
I am the grateful recipient of my own cherry blossom
ticker-tape parade, confetti and sunburst through clouds,
the cheering bystander trees, the ferry horn's
my own brass band.
I can't help delight, throw my arms up high!
Celebrate! Celebrate! This body, this life
my self.

—Libby Wagner, 2010

Some resources I love

Arbinger Institute, The. *Leadership and Self-Deception: Getting Out of the Box*. 2002.

Bennis, Warren. *Why Leaders Can't Lead: The Unconscious Conspiracy Continues*. 1997.

Bennis, Warren, Daniel Goleman and James O'Toole. *Transparency: Creating a Culture of Candor*. 2008.

Buckingham, Marcus. *First, Break All the Rules: What the World's Greatest Managers Do Differently*. 1999.

Clifton, Donald. *Soar With Your Strengths: A Simple Yet Revolutionary Philosophy of Business and Management*. 1995.

Covey, Stephen M.R. and Rebecca R. Merrill. *The Speed of Trust: The One Thing That Changes Everything*. 2008.

Elton, Chester and Adrian Gostick. *The Carrot Principle: How the Best Managers Use Recognition to Engage Their People, Retain Talent and Accelerate Performance*. 2009.

Flaum, J.P. "When it Comes to Business Leadership, Nice Guys Finish First: A GreenPeak Partners Study that Conventional Wisdom is Wrong—and that Leaders Who Possess Strong Soft Skills Perform Better at Driving Hard Results." 2010. www.greenpeakpartners.com.

Frankl, Viktor. *Man's Search for Meaning*. Special edition. 2006.

Goia, Dana. "Can Poetry Matter?" in *The Atlantic*, May 1991.

Goldberg, Natalie. *Writing Down the Bones: Freeing the Writer Within*. Special Edition. 2010.

Kahan, Seth. *Getting Change Right: How Leaders Transform Organizations from the Inside Out*. 2010.

Kramer, Roderick. "Rethinking Trust." *Harvard Business Review*. June 2009.

Lencioni, Patrick. *Overcoming the Five Dysfunctions of a Team: A Field Guide for Leaders, Managers and Facilitators*. 2005.

Oliver, Mary. *American Primitive*. 1983. (poems)

Roach, Michael, Lama Christy McNally and Michael Gordon. *Karmic Management: What Comes Around Goes Around in Your Business and Your Life*. 2009.

Selby, John. *Listening With Empathy: Creating Genuine Connections with Customers and Colleagues*. 2007.

Wagner, Libby. "Two Strategies for Success," American Management Association: *MWorld*. Fall 2007.

Weiss, Alan. *Thrive! Stop Wishing Your Life Away*. 2009.

Weyant, Bob. *Confronting Without Guilt or Conflict: How to Prepare and Deliver a Confrontation in a Way that Minimizes Risk, Conflict and Guilt*. 2009. 2nd Edition.

Wheatley, Margaret. *Leadership and The New Science*. 1994.

Whyte, David. *The Heart Aroused: Poetry and the Preservation of the Soul in Corporate America*. 1996.

Whyte, David. *The Three Marriages: Reimagining Work, Self & Relationship*. 2010.

Acknowledgements

It's nearly impossible to thank everyone who has supported me in the writing of this book and in the development of the ideas. Everyone says that, but it's true.

First, I must thank mentor and friend Bob Weyant and his wonderful wife Carol, whose work throughout the years created the foundations for the original Influencing Skills models and the years of work with clients and friends who tested and practiced to really make a difference in their courageous conversations. Thanks for your generosity and trust.

Second, I offer deep gratitude to my business mentor, coach, and thought-provocateur Alan Weiss, without whom it would've been impossible for a poet to make the transition to world-class business consultant. Thanks so much for your example and inspiration and for encouraging me to LIVE LARGE!

To Nance VanWinckel, poet and teacher, who not only helped me dive into language fearlessly, but who also sat with me in Mexico when I didn't know what to do after being terminated from my job and asked, "What would you do if you could do anything?" (along with dear writer friend Ann Clizer) Neither laughed when I told them my vision and both have delighted at my journey ever since.

To my Shameless Self-Promotion colleagues, Kim Wilkerson, Dr. Guido Quelle, and Chad Barr, whose brilliant minds and sense of humor continue to push me onward, ever shamelessly creating value for my clients and tooting my own horn.

To the Influencing Options Resource Partners and trainers who wholeheartedly teach these skills to their clients and mine, with gusto, commitment, and big doses of the Core Dimensions.

To my Million Dollar Consulting® compatriots, especially Stuart Cross, Phil Symchych, Lisa Bing, Wes Trochlil, Steve Ledgerwood, Pat Lynch, Bill Corbett, Seth Kahan, Simma Lieberman, Rob Nixon, Suzanne Bates, Dan Weedin, Katherine Radeka and ALL of the rest of you who've been so generous in your support and wisdom and we did "share some mighty fine wine" while we've traipsed the globe!

To Ken Lizotte who helped me navigate the book biz to find the perfect publisher for me . . . and to Eric Dobby at Global who just knew my book would have a global audience and has been a joy to work with. To David and Phillip who created amazing graphics from my pencil scribbles. Special thanks to designer Kevin O'Connor who, like all cool British men, says "brilliant" for the smallest things and makes me feel so grand!

To those who were willing to read the book draft and offer insightful comments and help: Kim, Pat, Maria, Mom, Phillip, David, Ken, Alan.

To every student, mentoree, and workshop participant I've had who endured my waxing on about Thoreau, Frankl, Shakespeare and Mary Oliver, and so much more: I always learned more than you did, I promise.

To my dear friends and blessed beings who just LOVE me: Gail, Shay, Shannon, Kim, Karla, April, Jann (and the crazy PC gals), Candy, Julie, Cathy, Tess, Diann, Deborah, Sharon, Kathianne, Freddie, Claudette, WBE women, Chad (who's as good as a girlfriend),

To my clients, especially those of the last few years, whose courageous work, vulnerability and good wisdom helped me write this book *for you* and all the while you were strengthening your teams, your organizations and your selves. You inspire me and honor me with our collaboration. Thanks especially to the leaders and teams of Gifts By Design, Community Health Care of Tacoma, Apex Facility Resources, Philips Healthcare Solution Center, Diageo, Spokane County Sheriff's Office, Colorado Community Health Care, First Creek Middle School, Family Health Care, Cascadia PM, Costco, D'Ewarts Representatives, Peninsula College and Avocent Corporation.

The biggest shout-out and deep gratitude to Phillip Bryant, who changed his own title to Director of Global Operations when indeed that's what he was doing. There's simply no way my business would've grown, developed or actually come to implementation without his help, his logic mind and his managing of me. He's freed me up to be my best poet-self as a businesswoman, and I am a better person for it.

To those whose inspiration and support go above and beyond in too many ways to list: my sister Missy, who ROCKS because she's a good friend, inspiring teacher, great mom, super wife and is willing to wear any funny hat for a photo with me. For my sister Karen, who still inspires and makes me laugh, and I know she would think this book was SO cool. My grandmother, LaVerne, who was bodacious and audacious and keeps showing up in my face in the mirror.

Index